SITTING ON
THE LAP OF
GOD

TIMOTHY MARK

SITTING ON THE LAP OF GOD

*Discover the Father
You've Always Longed For*

DEI VENTUS

Sitting on the Lap of God
© 2022 by Timothy Mark

DEI VENTUS

All rights reserved. Except for brief excerpts for review purposes, no part of this book may be reproduced or used in any form without written permission from the publisher.

For more information, visit timothymark.com

Unless otherwise noted, Scripture quotations are from The ESV® Bible (The Holy Bible, English Standard Version®), copyright © 2001 by Crossway, a publishing ministry of Good News Publishers. Used by permission. All rights reserved. Scripture quotations marked NLT are taken from Holy Bible, New Living Translation, copyright © 1996, 2004, 2015 by Tyndale House Foundation. Used by permission of Tyndale House Publishers, Inc., Carol Stream, Illinois 60188. All rights reserved. Scripture quotations marked KJV are taken from the The Holy Bible, King James Version (KJV), public domain. Scripture quotations marked NIV are taken from the Holy Bible, New International Version®, NIV®. Copyright © 1973, 1978, 1984, 2011 by Biblica, Inc.™ Used by permission of Zondervan. All rights reserved worldwide. www.zondervan.com The "NIV" and "New International Version" are trademarks registered in the United States Patent and Trademark Office by Biblica, Inc.™

Library of Congress Control Number: 2021918626
ISBN: 978-1-7379102-0-6 (paperback)

Edited by Jennifer Huber
Cover design by Spencer Fuller, Faceout Studio
Cover image by Tony Myshlyaev, Stocksy
Interior image by Denise Jans, Unsplash

Permissions and credit lines for quoted material may be found in the back of the book under "Notes."

The author has attempted to recreate experiences from his life based on his recollection of events. To protect privacy, in some instances, names of individuals and places have been changed, along with identifying characteristics.

This book is not intended as a substitute for the advice of a medical or mental health professional. The reader should consult a professional counselor or physician in matters relating to his/her addiction, mental health, and any symptoms that may require diagnosis or medical attention. This book should not be used as a substitute for professional care.

Published by Dei Ventus
www.DeiVentus.com

First Edition

3 5 7 9 10 8 6 4 2

Contents

Preface	ix
1. THE UNIVERSAL ACHE	1
Hamster Wheels	2
Where Fatherlessness Begins	5
2. THE FATHER WHO ACHES FOR US	9
The Father-Shaped Hole	10
The Father Who Wants to Dwell with His Kids	13
3. SEARCHING FOR A FATHER	17
4. THE HAPPINESS OF THE FATHER	27
The Happiness of God	30
The Pursuit of Happiness	32
5. SEPARATED FROM THE FATHER	39
Separated from the Father	41
Reconnecting with the Father	43
6. BECOMING A CHILD AGAIN	47
Embracing Childhood	49
Giving Up Trying to Be a Good Christian	50
Giving Up Trying to Serve God	52
7. CONVERSATIONS WITH THE FATHER	57
Why God Created Prayer	58
The Parable of the Father and the Phone	60
The Parable of the Awkward Conversation	61
Avoiding Routine	64
8. LEARNING TO LISTEN	69
Hearing the Voice of the Father	71
Finding Confirmation	73
9. TAKING BACK OUR IDENTITY	79
Finding Our Identity	81
Children of the Father God	84
The Father of Love and the Father of Lies	85

10. SURRENDERING TO THE FATHER'S LOVE	91
The Great Mystery	94
11. THE FATHER WHO HEALS OUR SHAME	99
Coming Home	101
12. LEARNING TO BE STILL	109
What Matters Most	112
You Make Me Happy	114
What Makes the Father Happy?	116
13. EMBRACING OUR WEAKNESSES	123
Sharing Our Struggles	124
Confession within Community	129
14. THE VIEW FROM HIS LAP	133
The Peace that Guards Us	137
Child's Toys	138
15. GRIEVING WHAT WAS LOST	143
A Place of Hope	146
16. RECEIVING AND GIVING GRACE	153
Undeserved Grace	154
Flinch	158
17. THE WILDERNESS OF TESTING	163
The Wilderness of Testing	165
Will We Meet Our Needs on Our Own?	166
18. ASKING THE HARD QUESTIONS	171
Will We Trust the Father?	172
Will We Let Go of Unhealthy Desires?	175
The Search for Significance	177
19. DISCOVERING A NEW FAMILY	183
The Gathering	186
20. SITTING ON THE LAP OF GOD	191
Transformation	194
The Invitation	196
Acknowledgments	199
Appendix	201
Notes	207

*Is there something at the end of life?
Is there more? Can you reach communion
with someone or something that voids the
loneliness that we all feel? I don't know.
I pose it as a question.*

—William Shatner
Actor

Preface

I feel as if I've discovered a secret that has been hiding in plain sight for two thousand years. This secret changed my life. In the following pages, I'll share the secret with you. I promise that if you read this to the end, you will discover for yourself the secret I have found.

I travel solo in this journey to wholeness, to the filling of a long-held ache, but I am not alone. There are thousands, no millions, of us on this journey. I look back to you, encouraging you on, as I continue to press forward. I sweep my arm toward you, the arc urging you to come to me, to come alongside me, to walk *with* me on this journey to the Father's love. From higher up the path, I shout to you. Hurry! You can't imagine what I've seen. You have to experience this.

And so I set pen to paper to attempt to describe the journey thus far. I am a reluctant expert in this saga. It is not a story I wanted to write. Writing my story picks scabs off old wounds I thought were healed. Writing reveals healing still needed, forgiveness and grace reapplied like a salve. Forgiveness to others whose actions made my ache more profound. Forgiveness for myself for ways I responded. Grace for myself even when I do not deserve it, and yes, grace for others who may not deserve it either.

"Fatherless" is a broad term we use to describe the effect of an absent or abusive father. Definitions of *absent* or *abusive* run the gamut from unintentional neglect to willful abandonment, from harsh words spoken in anger to physical harm requiring medical attention. All pick at a natural hole in our lives, opening the hollow broader and broader until, like a black hole in the universe, it sucks everything in our lives into it. And often, we feel stuck, unable to move forward.

My curiosity took me to the National Center for Fathering, where statistics greatly troubled me. More disturbing was the seeming lack of a long-term solution. Our attempts to solve the crisis didn't seem to work. There had to be a better way.

That's when I began to wonder if the solution was in the spirit realm, not the physical realm. Certainly, experiences that occurred in our lives were in the physical realm. But what if these physical manifestations of fatherlessness were an expression of a spiritual issue? Like a morning fog lifting off a forest meadow, I saw for the first time how the Father God created us to be his children. I saw his face smiling at me when the realization dawned upon me. The Father God wants to dwell with his children. The Father wants to heal the ache.

For centuries, God was considered unapproachable, violent, to be feared. Then, in the region of Galilee in Israel, a humble carpenter declared that God was his father. The God of Israel, their God, was his father. Further infuriating the religious leaders, he declared he was the only Son of this Father God. The establishment roiled. Eventually, they killed him for his claim. They thought they could silence him. But what was once far away was now brought near. Truth was revealed. The Father God wanted his kids back.

Just as then, forces today try to hide this truth from you and me. Why? Because this truth can transform our lives. And some don't want to see that happen. A hidden war strives to separate us from our Father. How can we possibly succeed?

Consider the following pages as a map for our journey. As we walk together, I'll share my story with my flaws and weaknesses on display. But, more importantly, I'll take you to my favorite shelters along the way, places of rest where I discovered the Father I've always longed for. I'll show you how fatherlessness is a part of our human DNA. And where once we felt alone, we discover community. We are not alone, after all. And because this is a journey, I'll also share helpful directions for you to find healing for addiction, pornography, unhealthy relationships, and more – issues I've wrestled with along the way.

Explore this secret path with me. Find fullness where once was emptiness. End the weary cycle once and for all.

Our journey begins with a growing awareness of an unsettled ache in our lives. The signpost at the head of the path reads, "Fatherless." It points the way to an uncertain, dimly lit path. Previous wounds choke the trail from either side, their thorns tearing into flesh as we press through. This expedition is not going to be easy. The course is not straight and smooth. It is broken, crooked, and sometimes feels like it is winding back to where we began. But ultimately, the path leads to the lap of a loving God, where we discover the Father we've always longed for.

Come, the light is dawning. It is time to begin.

If it's success, you can never get enough of that. I realized that it doesn't stop. It keeps calling you. It's like a drug. It's a hamster wheel, and you're never satisfied.

—Bruno Mars
Singer

Chapter 1

The Universal Ache

It is helpful for you to know I walk *with* you on this journey. I write this as much for myself as for you. I write from a place of experience. It wasn't until recently I discovered the root of my concerns. I know how the Universal Ache feels. I imagine you already know the place of which I speak. If not, allow me to explain.

We all experience this pain to one degree or another. It is the Universal Ache. Many describe it as a feeling of emptiness. It appears as a sense of longing, a haunting loneliness. Something is not quite right. And no matter what we do, somehow it resurfaces, clawing its way back, gasping for air. Our attempts to fill the ache manifest themselves in many troubling areas of our lives. We try many things to fill that space. Even as you read these words, it is likely a situation in your life comes to mind. You suspect a particular behavior might not be helpful. Unhealed, we experience a realm of disfunction. On the surface, many of these behaviors seem helpful in filling the void. But in the end, none satisfy. None.

Hamster Wheels

Our relationships feel unsettled. Some try to fill the void with a cycle of marriage, divorce, and remarriage, hoping somehow it will be different with each new relationship. If only someone loved us for who we are. Unconditionally. Without reservation. Surely there is someone out there who can meet the need in our lives. We swipe our way through online dating apps, searching for "The One." We spend the weekend hooking up, hoping to fill the void, only to find emptiness walking us home on the walk of shame.

Others try to comfort the ache with another glass of chardonnay or another hit of a prescription drug. We try to numb the Universal Ache. But moments of ecstasy are washed away with feelings of guilt and shame. So we pour another glass or take another pill to soothe the sense of guilt. The downward cycle begins. Some, desperate to fill the void, even risk prison and public shame with the use of illegal drugs.

Some try to fill the void with success. We work longer hours, we work harder, scraping our way to the top only to reach the pinnacle and find the trophy case is empty. We expect accolades but hear only the sound of bare, cold wind. The pursuit of happiness doesn't lead to happiness. It only leads to more pursuit. On and on it goes. If only we could make a million, we would be happy. Then we become millionaires only to discover we are not satisfied after all. We buy a nicer house in a nicer neighborhood, but emptiness finds where we live. The problems in our previous residence were forwarded to our new home before we even had a chance to submit a change of address.

Some turn to social media. Surely this will satisfy, so we strive for more followers, more likes, more shares. We scroll endlessly through feeds, unconsciously trying to find the post that may give some relief to the ache. We photoshop our lives to infer we have found the golden ticket, but it is a shallow, empty vanity of vanities. We check our feed to see how many likes our post received. We read the comments to see how much we are loved. We check shares to see if perhaps our post will go viral. But it never satisfies. Never.

Some turn to pornography for relief, hiding images on their phone, even risking losing a job by downloading porn at work. Whatever it takes to keep the dopamine flowing. Images that once brought the rush of arousal no longer interest. So we click further and further down the rabbit hole of shame, fueled by a lust for more dopamine to soothe our souls.

Some turn to food to comfort the ache. We even created an entire category of food called comfort food. We are hungry to fill the void. Instinctively, we feel unsatisfied in life, so we reach for another cookie, another slice of pie to fill the longing. But it never satisfies. Health issues follow. Recognizing we have a problem but not clear how to solve it, we lose weight, gain it back, and lose it again, rebounding our way through life.

Some realize food will never satisfy, so they turn to health and fitness to fill the void. We work out, chasing an image we saw on the cover of a magazine or a social media feed, never quite achieving the desired look. This impulse drives us to exercise not from a desire to *be* healthy but to *look* healthy, to have the perfect physique. Yet, strangely, even healthy obsessions are unhealthy. So we clothe our identities in a layer of flawless skin and toned muscles, hoping no one will notice how perfectly empty we are inside.

Some try to buy their way out of the despair. But no matter how much we buy, it never fills the hole. We order happiness online, and a box is delivered to our doorstep the following day. We open the box only to discover it is empty. So we order more packages. We fill our homes to overflowing. Then we rent storage space to store the items that no longer satisfy. We park our new car in the driveway because there is no room in the garage. Our debt load crushes us, leading to even more tension. The garage is full, but our lives remain empty.

Some try to soothe the ache with a life of adventure, trolling the globe for the next buzz of adrenaline. We travel the world, searching for the magic elixir. But like any other drug, adrenaline never satisfies. So we explore further, probing the darkness for a higher level of intensity, the next item on the bucket list, the one that will finally appease our desire to be filled.

We may even try religion. We work hard to follow all the rules. We commit to the program. But in the end, we feel empty and burned out. We attend church every weekend. We follow the service order religiously. We sit when it is time to sit. We stand when it is time to stand. We put our money into the offering plate. We listen to the message. Then we walk out the door and return home to our empty lives. It frustrates us that our lives look no different from our neighbor who stayed home to watch NASCAR. We question why we still feel empty when religion was supposed to fulfill us. The ache remains.

Sadly, once we discover the path we have chosen does not satisfy, we try a different approach in a vain attempt to fill the void. But it never works. So we spend our lives cycling through the process, never finding fulfillment. Never. Always the ache returns.

For most of my life, I've known this ache deeply. It was an itch I could not scratch, always just out of reach. I thought that if I tried hard enough, eventually, I could reach it. But my efforts only left me tired, weary, exhausted. Seasons of depression filtered in and out like tides. At my low points, it was difficult to get out of bed. A weariness clung to me, weighing me down, making any movement tiresome. The success of songs like "Somewhere Over the Rainbow" or "I Still Haven't Found What

I'm Looking For" should have been a clue that my condition was universal, yet still I felt alone.

Where Fatherlessness Begins

It may surprise you to discover this Universal Ache has less to do with how we were raised and more to do with our DNA. Fatherlessness is a condition we inherit from the generation before us. It is part of our DNA. Often our family circumstances exasperate the issue. Childhood trauma stalks us throughout the remainder of our lives. But our Universal Ache can be traced back to a man and woman who lived in a beautiful place called the Garden of Eden.

In the beginning, God created Adam and Eve and placed them in this garden. Of all the things God created, humans were the only beings he made for which he intended to have a relationship. The Bible says God actually walked with Adam and Eve in the cool of the evening. He intended to be a father to his children. He wanted to dwell with them. He was their Father God.

In the garden, life was perfect. There was no Universal Ache. There was only the fullness of an ideal relationship with the Father. Adam and Eve had no needs. They navigated their days tending the garden, naming the animals, enjoying the fullness of their relationship with the Father. The presence of the Father was a treasure to them. When they spent time with the Father, it was in the closeness of his intimate love.

Now a unique tree stood in the garden, the tree of the knowledge of good and evil. Everything in the garden was freely available to Adam and Eve except this one tree. Of this tree, they were not to eat the fruit. The consequence was severe. "In the day you eat of it," the Father said, "you will surely die."

Seasons came and went, and Adam and Eve relished their

lives in the garden. Until one fateful day that changed everything.

A beguiling serpent also lived in the garden, and he hated the Father. He wanted nothing more than to destroy the relationship the Father had with his children. So he plotted and patiently waited for the opportunity to strike.

Finally, it happened. "Wouldn't you be happy if you ate from the tree of the knowledge of good and evil," the enemy whispered to Eve. For a moment, Eve pondered the thought. Perhaps the serpent was right. The tree was good for food, and it looked beautiful. Wisdom was a good thing, right? So she picked a piece of the fruit and brought it to her lips. The fruit was sweet and firm. A momentary rush swept over her as the juice trickled down her chin. She handed a piece to Adam, and he ate as well.

The act opened their eyes in a way they had not experienced before. Immediately they understood what they had done was wrong. For the first time in their lives, they felt the sting of shame. For the first time, they realized they were naked. They tried to cover up the best they could, beginning a process we still follow today.

A strange, new ache opened in their hearts. They felt it in the pit of their stomachs at the moment they swallowed the forbidden fruit. For sin had entered the garden, and fatherlessness had begun.

A lot of people say that there's a big God-shaped hole in your heart and when that's filled you really are satisfied. And I think that's where I am right now.

—Alice Cooper
Singer-songwriter

Chapter 2

The Father Who Aches for Us

Heaven held its breath, and a deathly silence descended on the room. The Father saw what had happened in the garden and knew the gravity of the moment. Sin always separates. Always. Now, this sin separated him from his precious children, and the thought wrecked him. From the beginning, all he had wanted was to dwell with his kids. Nothing more. He wanted nothing from them but to be with them, to enjoy communion with them, to sit with them and enjoy the beauty of the garden together. Now, for the first time, he was separated from his children. His heart ached to reunite with them. He looked over at his son and, for a moment, their eyes met. Without speaking a word, Jesus slowly nodded.

It was a costly move, this small moment in the garden. Because the penalty for sin was death and now someone would have to pay the price.

Someone would have to die.

The Father Shaped Hole

From that singular moment in the garden, fatherlessness began. The Father God created you and me to be his children. From the beginning, he intended to father us. Wholly. Perfectly bathed in his love, washed in his presence. Then sin came and ruined it all.

From that first moment of sin, a hole opened up in our lives. We received it when we were born, and we pass it on to the next generation every time we give birth. This spiritual condition manifests itself in our physical world. It is the Father-shaped hole in our lives, the Universal Ache. The Father God created this void in our lives, and he made it to be filled by him alone. Even the best dad cannot wholly satisfy the void in our lives created on that fateful day. For we are fallen, each of us.

Because we are fallen creatures, just like Adam and Eve, we instinctively know when we have done wrong. We don't require a list printed out saying, "Do this. Don't do that." We sense it when we are wrong. And like Adam and Eve, we try to cover up when we've blown it. It is our nature. It is in our DNA. We carry this fallen nature within us. Broken. We long to be whole. We long to be restored in the relationship with the Father God, but our sin separates us from him.

Through the centuries, the Father God longed to reconnect with his children. To dwell with his kids is what truly made him happy. Not seeing us following rules and not watching us going through religious rituals to appease him somehow. No, the one thing that genuinely made the Father happy was to be with his kids. But the only way that could happen is if someone paid the penalty for their sin. Remember, someone would have to die.

From the beginning, the Father knew this would happen and put in place a plan so he could reconnect with his kids. His precious son Jesus would pay the penalty for our sin. As the Son of God, he was the perfect one to do it. So finally, the Father gave the world his son.

Jesus left his position in heaven at the side of the Father and was born to a teenage girl in an unremarkable town. But what a remarkable baby! There was no moment when he disobeyed. No backtalk. No crying when he didn't get his way. Always willing to share his toys. Full of love. Perfect.

As he grew, religious leaders marveled at his understanding of Scripture. In his teens, he spent afternoons in the Temple, dialoging with the teachers.

And the miracles. Oh, the miracles were the thing that amazed everyone. As an adult, he healed the blind. People born unable to walk stood and leapt at his command. Everyone who came to him found healing long sought. Even the demons obeyed him. One time he raised a man from the dead four days after he had died. Crowds grew. Thousands sat for his teaching.

But with all this, the one thing that infuriated the religious leaders the most was that Jesus claimed to be the Son of God. He dared to refer to God as his father. And not just once or twice. Everywhere he went, he peppered the idea into his conversations. "The Father wants to be with his children. The Father wants to forgive you for your sins. The Father wants you to know him on a personal level." The religious leaders were enraged. They had built the whole structure of their religion on limiting access to God. They were the gatekeepers. Now, masses of people were following this uncouth rebel.

For a time, they tried sending their lawyers to catch him in heresy. But each time, Jesus humiliated them with his replies. The ordinary people, once held tightly in the grip of the religious establishment, now laughed at the Scribes and the Pharisees. Their rage grew.

The religious establishment had an awkward but cozy relationship with the government. Now, they manipulated it to their advantage. They met with the governor, who agreed to arrest Jesus. Finally, under the cloak of darkness, they raided Jesus' camp. Everyone fled. But Jesus willingly surrendered to the authorities.

It is not clear if the religious leaders intended to have Jesus killed or to have him arrested and put out of sight until things cooled down. But, in the end, he was sentenced to death by crucifixion. They condemned a man who had never harmed anyone to die a hideous death. Those who once followed him closely now scattered like rats when someone turns on a light. He endured alone.

They beat him, mocked him, and spit in his face. They whipped him until the flesh on his back shredded into ribbons. They paraded him through the city streets like a circus animal. And where once crowds had shouted his name in adoration, they now jeered as he stumbled to his execution.

They humiliated him, stripping him naked. They nailed his hands and feet to the rough-hewn wooden cross and stood it up like a trophy for all to see. They laughed as the cross thudded into place in the hole dug from the rocky ground, the force ripping flesh off his body.

Some who had followed him closely now stood at a distance and watched the scene unfold. They had thought he had come to save the world. But now, his barely breathing carcass was hanging on a cross. It was not the end they expected. The loss was crushing.

On the cross, Jesus had never experienced pain like this. He endured for hours. But now, his entire body was shutting down. He struggled for every breath. He could hardly breathe. With profound effort, he raised himself one final time, drawing a breath deep into his lungs. Then, with arms outstretched, he lifted his face to the heavens.

The people gathered to watch the spectacle were shocked

when he slowly smiled. Pure joy flooded over him. Where once he felt pain, he now felt ecstasy. Death was closing in. His body was giving way. His final breath shared a wonder more profound than anyone could understand. His voice startled the gathered witnesses as slowly yet firmly he shouted.

"IT... IS... FINISHED!"

The Son of God died. The price for all sin was paid.

The Father could dwell with his kids again.

The Father Who Wants to Dwell with His Kids

The Father God wants to spend time with his kids. The story begins in the Garden of Eden, but it does not end there. Indeed, if we look to the opposite end of the Bible, we find the Father dwelling with his children again. The Bible says that at the end of all things, God will create a new heaven and a new earth, and the Father God will dwell with us. We will be his kids, and God himself will abide with us.

The Father wants to dwell with his kids. In the beginning, it was so. In the end, it will be again.

This discovery that the entire Bible is bookended with stories of a father who wants to dwell with his children made me ponder what I should focus on in the in-between. Both stories reveal a father who loves spending time with his kids. Both instances are examples of what a relationship with the Father looks like when it is not affected by sin. Both are illustrations of the ideal relationship with the Father.

Unfortunately, I live in the here and now. Sin profoundly affects my world. How then should I live? What should I focus on today? What should my relationship with the Father God look like in the years between the Garden of Eden and the new heaven and earth? What if I made it my sole focus to spend time with the Father as if I lived in the Garden of Eden? What if I spent my days dwelling with him as I will at the end of all time? How would *that* kind of relationship with him look?

I began questioning everything I thought I knew about being a Christian. It was difficult to drill down beneath the traditions of the Church to discover the foundational truths of the Bible. Much of what my religious experience taught me was an interpretation of what the previous generation thought was correct. I looked back at the reforms organized religion made through history. In general, the reforms addressed shortfalls in the practice of the day. Few reforms looked back to where it all began, to the life and times of Jesus. When I looked closely at the writings in the Bible, I saw little similarity between the teachings of Jesus and the religious practice I experienced now.

And so I looked at my life and relationship with the Father God with new eyes. What if I stripped away the practice of religion and focused solely on spending time with the Father? It seemed unthinkable yet intriguing. What if I started at the beginning, like Adam and Eve before sin entered the world? I knew it wasn't possible to have a perfect, sin-free relationship with him, but at least I could focus on what the Father thought was important.

The path grows more apparent with each step we take. We begin to see how much we need to change. Slowly we see the price the Father paid on our behalf. With each hesitant step, we begin to understand the path to the lap of God always leads through the cross. It is through the cross we are born anew. Our new life begins.

We must be born again, for the Father cannot father us if we are not willing to be his children.

I struggled a long time with not only bouts of depression I've had, but also things that have happened to me earlier when I was a teenager that colored me as an adult. I struggled a long time to just express myself.

—Dwayne Johnson
"The Rock," Actor

Chapter 3

Searching for a Father

My journey to the lap of God did not start well. Along the way, I missed opportunities that could have changed the trajectory of my life. As a result, many regrets haunt me. How I would love a do-over. But while I cannot go back, I am hopeful I can guide you down paths that will help you avoid the mistakes I made as I fought to find a way to wholeness.

My story began in a small farming community in southern Michigan. Five hundred sixty-eight residents called the hamlet home. There was no stoplight, only a four-way stop at the heart of the village. When a farmer moved a tractor between fields, traffic would back up on the two-lane roads that fed into the town. Otherwise, typically the streets were empty. Old maples stood like sentinels on both sides of the road, shading the roadway with a canopy of red and yellow leaves in the fall. We lived on Main Street and had a cornfield in our backyard. Beyond the field, there were woods. As a child, I spent countless hours exploring those fields and woods. Often, I packed a lunch in the morning and let my mother know I would be gone until dinner.

My favorite memories from childhood remain tucked away in those woods.

What no one knew was that I went to the woods to escape. In the woods, no one spoke harshly to me. In the woods, no one struck me in anger. In the woods, no one belittled me. The woods became my refuge, the trees and meadows my Garden of Eden. I discovered Jack-in-the-Pulpit, their trumpet-shaped blooms straining toward sunlight from boggy bottom loam. I could identify a dozen species of birds by their call or flight pattern. Once I unknowingly stumbled into the center of a herd of whitetail deer bedded down in a high-grass meadow. When I paused to sip from my water bottle, the woods exploded with deer running in all directions. My heart nearly stopped within my chest. It was exhilarating. I always managed to find my way back to the house before dark. But when I peeled off my shoes on the concrete slab of the back porch and opened the backdoor of the house, it was with a sense of regret.

Like many midwestern towns, our village had three churches: a Methodist church and two Baptist churches. There are always two Baptist churches in a city. Their method of multiplication is to divide and form two from one. The church I attended was the Independent Baptist church. It began as a split from the other Baptist church around the corner. We were independent of any association with any other church and proud of it. I attended only because my dad was the pastor. As a pastor's kid, I was in church every time the doors were open, Sunday morning, Sunday night, and Wednesday night at a minimum. When revival speakers were in town, we attended nightly. Eventually, I figured out I could fake being sick to stay home. Stomach cramps were my go-to illness. There was no test that could prove I did not have stomach distress.

In those days, the community held the pastor's family in high esteem. But the village also held us to a higher standard.

My fun-loving nature frequently got me into trouble. In school, I was a cut-up. I had a quick wit and a sharp tongue, a skill my teachers rarely appreciated. Once a teacher pulled me out of class, wagged her finger in my face, and sternly told me a pastor's kid shouldn't act like that. It seemed unfair at the time. I was no different than any other child. But community expectations in a small town don't have to be fair. They just need to be followed.

Our two-story brick home, built in the late 1800s, was set on a quarter-acre lot filled with mature, sprawling maple trees. A wide porch with sturdy, white columns graced the front of the house. On one end of the porch, a porch swing hung from the ceiling. But all was not well within our brick façade.

While the community held us in high regard, behind closed doors, a different scene unfolded. I have few recollections of happy moments within those walls. I could never quite please my dad. I know he did his best, but he had his own struggles. I avoided him in an attempt to prevent the sting of a derogatory comment or worse.

Often, discipline was administered harshly, without grace or love. I avoided the belt and the board as much as I could. I learned to escape to the woods when my dad was upset. There were plenty of times I earned discipline from a rebellious action. But my recollection is one of avoiding angry incidents that felt little like discipline and more like abuse. My child's heart fractured into shards; the hollows scraped bare.

In the summertime, the heat and humidity made for muggy days and sweltering nights. The hum of a box fan was nearly always in the background. With no air-conditioner, we opened the double-hung windows to let the breeze flow through the screens. My childish mind imagined this might help our family situation. Perhaps if the neighbors heard the things that were going on, they might intercede. To this day, I wonder what they thought when they heard us fighting. Our neighbors never said a word. Perhaps behind closed doors and windows, they were fighting themselves. Still, the thought of exposing our chaos seemed hopeful.

One bright spot in my youth was my childhood dog. His name was Shawn, given to him by the neighbor who gave him to us as a puppy. He was a German Shepherd-Norwegian Elkhound mix. His heavy coat carried the gray and black pattern of the Norwegian Elkhound, and his piercing eyes revealed the keen intellect of a German Shepherd. I loved that dog. We got him when I was six years old. He was the family dog, but I treated him as if he were solely my own. He was sensitive. When I was happy, he was pleased. Sometimes when there was chaos in the house, I would escape to the barn where we kept him. I would sit next to him when I was crying, and he would nuzzle in, pressing into my side as if he understood. Unfortunately, he died on my twentieth birthday. Alone in my room, I buried my face in my pillow so no one could hear and wept. I still miss that dog. In a strange way that dog helped fill the Father void I felt as a boy.

I played little league baseball for two years. During practice, I hit the ball out of the park. But an odd thing happened during actual games. Insecurity overwhelmed me. I never got a hit in a game. Not once. One time, my bat connected with the ball, and I thought the drought was finally over. But the ball went foul down the right baseline. I stood at the plate, my bat dangling by my side, and watched the ball pull to the right. I quit shortly after that. It wasn't fun anymore. I saved my mitt, safely hidden away in a box. It is a child-sized leather mitt with my name written on the wrist strap in black ink. I have carried it with me for almost fifty years, move after move, a haunting reminder that I was never good enough. I suspect I save it in hopes that someday I can relive those moments and finally succeed.

Actions left hidden emotional scars long after the physical pain was gone. Harsh words ground into my spirit like sand in a cut. They continued to speak from somewhere deep in my soul, droning on like a song on autorepeat. I replayed the words, hoping I might find resolution and healing by doing so, but it only served to open the wounds anew. Publicly, of course. I rarely spoke of these things.

In the strict religious environment in which I grew up, how you looked mattered. Following rules mattered. I became adept at playing the part, saying just the right words, and smiling while I was crying inside. I even practiced my smile in the mirror so I could get it perfect. I nearly perfected the art of the façade. I instinctively knew how to dress the part and play the role. I was fun to be around. In high school, I was on the homecoming court. I had a quick wit, often sprinkling in profanity for effect. The f-bomb was not out of bounds. I smiled and made people laugh, and no one had any idea my home life was such a mess. My interior world was broken. But on the outside, I had it all together. The façade was the only thing that mattered. Never let your guard down. Always be the positive one. Always smile.

My first exposure to pornography occurred when I was too young to understand what I had seen. I was nine or ten years old. At a park down the street from our home, someone had ripped pages out of a porn magazine and hung them in the branches of a scrub brush on the back edge of the park. We discovered the images while we were playing. Deep inside, a strange feeling surged through me. The fire was lit. It smoldered within me from that moment on. In junior high, my brother and I had a porn magazine hidden in our shared bedroom, buried beneath puzzle boxes in the bottom of a dresser drawer. It was accessible anytime. In those images, I escaped the pain I was experiencing in life. At the time, I had no understanding of how destructive porn would eventually become. I did not know about sex addiction. It just felt better than what I was experiencing in the rest of my world.

My first forays into dating life revealed more problems. Needing to be perfect has its downside. I evaluated a girl based on how I would look beside her if she were my girlfriend. I had little understanding of love at even a basic level. I only knew I had to be perfect to be accepted. This I understood. If only I could be perfect, then maybe I could feel loved. Neither happened.

I went to college, and the woods faded away in the rearview mirror as the car pulled from the driveway. While I missed the woods of my childhood, I found ways to replace my time there. I could escape the pain of life in other ways.

The conservative Christian university I attended held similar tenets to how my parents raised me. It was familiar. Follow the rules, and everything will work out fine. So I followed the rules. I became a leader on campus. I won awards for Christian service. On the outside, I was the poster child for conservative religion. Inside, not so much. My skewed approach to dating continued, and it always ended poorly.

On the outside, my life looked perfect. But profound insecurity still haunted me. There was always something missing. I never felt like I belonged to the brotherhood of men. I wasn't strong enough. I wasn't athletic enough. I was not enough.

After college, I returned home to our tiny outpost and got a job at a local automotive parts factory. I began as an illustrator in the Quality Control department and worked my way into management. I felt promoted past my skill set, unqualified, and terrified I would be exposed. When I straightened my tie in the mirror, a small boy looked back at me, belittled and wounded. Finally, I quit.

I had some experience in the music industry and some skills on keys, so I began a career as a musician. My ability to create a façade was perfect for a performance-based career. I understood how to play the part. I instinctively knew how to give people what they wanted. I performed instrumental concerts on the piano in rural churches in my dad's circle of friends, using arrangements of classic hymns. Slowly my circle of influence grew, and I began doing concerts in multiple nearby states.

I also had some skills in writing music. I wrote my first lyric when I was in college. As my music career grew, I transitioned from doing instrumental concerts to becoming a singer/songwriter. At that time, many traditional churches banned Contemporary Christian Music (CCM). This style of music was a problem with some of the conservative churches I served. But CCM was the future. Artists like Keith Green, Amy Grant, and Michael W. Smith forged the path. Musically, it varied little from pop radio. Lyrically, it focused more on Christian themes. But the drums and electric guitar were problematic in my dad's circles. I produced an album of original contemporary Christian songs. I gave a copy to my parents, longing for their approval. It was months before my dad found time to listen to it. I imagine it was hard for him to accept. But I wanted his approval nonetheless. It was the equivalent of a toddler presenting his father with a scrawled crayon drawing only to have the father set it aside with a promise to look at it sometime in the future. I waited to hear what he would say, hoping for some approval. But it was not meant to be.

I thought if I could be successful, it might fill the void. So I pursued radio play. I wrote press releases to get my name in newspapers. My circle of influence expanded across the United States and Canada with occasional trips overseas. I started getting invitations to speak, a novelty for me, and I accepted. As a speaker, I began to get invitations to larger and larger events. All of it fed an unhealthy desire for significance. All of it was a façade of a successful ministry built on the frame of a small, wounded child still longing for healing. Always smile. Never let them see you cry.

In private moments, far from the platform and stage, I was lonely. The Father-shaped hole within me continued to grow. Unable to foster healthy relationships, I focused on work and career. But it was never enough. Occasionally, I medicated with porn to relieve the pain. I tried anything to fill the void. I followed my dreams. I sought adventure and dreamed of travel in Antarctica. I bought a home near the beach, spending the evenings fishing for dinner. I even bought a sailboat and lived aboard.

But, no matter what I tried, I felt empty. I could never entirely heal. There was always a part of me trying to dab the wound, hoping it would finally scab over tomorrow.

If only I understood the principles I'm sharing with you, how different my life could have been.

For when I discovered the secret, everything changed.

*I wish I had had a father who
was around and involved.*

—Barack Obama
44th President of the United States

*The gateway to life is very
narrow and the road is difficult,
and only a few ever find it.*

—Jesus

Chapter 4

The Happiness of the Father

While growing up, the church I attended seated around a hundred and fifty people when full, which it rarely, if ever was. Typically, forty to fifty folks from the village attended on a given Sunday. In the sweltering heat of August, we cranked open the windows lining the sides of the auditorium to provide a cross breeze, but it did little to keep the back of my starched white shirt from sticking to the hard wooden pew. I wore a tie like all good Independent Baptists did and a thread-bare suit handed down through four boys in another church family and then my older brother before finally hanging in my closet. (When eventually I outgrew it, we burned it in our burn barrel behind the barn, a moment I particularly relished.) We sang from a hymnbook which I balanced on the back of the pew in front of me. Special music was a mixed blessing. The talent pool was small. Best efforts were rewarded with hearty amens, even if the performance wasn't particularly good. We were ahead of our time in awarding participation trophies. Cutting edge.

New hymns like "Mansion over the Hilltop" pushed the envelope in our little orthodox bastion. Written by a traveling evangelist named Ira Stanphill in 1949, the song was a staple of early Southern Gospel artists who visited our church. The lyrics cast a romantic view of heaven, a place where a mansion waits for us just over the hillside. It has sold over two million copies to date. Elvis even recorded it. The congregation sang it with gusto. Women got misty-eyed. The hope of a nicer home than we all currently lived in overwhelmed us. I wistfully imagined my mansion would have air conditioning.

But now, forty-some years later, I question the lyrics. If the song is true, then heaven is a place that is all about our happiness, and I suspect that is not the case. Presumably, the basis for the song comes from a passage in the Bible. Ira Stanphill, the songwriter, likely read from the King James Version of the Bible, the same version we used in our church, which quotes Jesus as saying: "In my Father's house are many mansions; if it were not so, I would have told you. I go to prepare a place for you. And if I go and prepare a place for you, I will come again, and receive you unto myself; that where I am, there ye may be also." Unfortunately, the translators of this version interpreted the original Greek word for *dwelling* or *abode* as *mansion*, likely not the best choice of words. Newer versions corrected this translation error.

"I am going to prepare a place for you," Jesus says. But there is more to it. He explains he is preparing room for us so that eventually he can bring us home with him, to live with him where he lives. Where does Jesus live? At the right hand of the Father in heaven. The whole point of his going and preparing a place for us is so that we can be with him and with the Father. The point of heaven is not beautiful mansions, harps, and crowns for our enjoyment. It is our dwelling with the Father! Finally, the Father reconnects with his kids. Finally, once and for all time, he dwells with us as he intended to do from the beginning. At that moment, I suspect we will not care about what kind of house we live in, whether it has air conditioning or whether we have a harp or wear a crown.

I can hear Southern Gospel artists rolling over in their graves. But, in reality, the story of the Bible says that the end of all things is the happiness of God. We interpret the Bible through the lens of the happiness of God, not through the lens of our happiness. Jesus' words make sense when we understand he frames them in the happiness of the Father. The Father wants to dwell with his kids. Dwelling with his kids makes him happy! So he makes room for them in his dwelling place. Jesus encourages us when he says, "I am going to prepare a place for you so that you can dwell face to face with the Father, just as I do." Done. Drop the mic. Give him a hearty "Amen," or, at the very least, a participation trophy.

Somewhere the Methodists down the street whisper a sigh of relief that at least they were not Baptists. But focusing on our happiness is not unique to Baptists. The promise of happiness saturates our teachings across denominational boundaries. If we are not careful, it seeps into our core beliefs. "God wants me to be happy," we say. "So surely since this makes me happy, it must be okay." Nothing could be further from the truth.

The truth is the story of the Bible is all about the happiness of the Father. Sometimes it makes him happy to do nice things for his kids. At other times it makes him happy to see us shaped to look a little more like his son Jesus. He allows problems and trials to press and mold us into Jesus' image. In those moments, we are not happy. No, the process is challenging. We push back. We don't like the pressure. But in the end, the Bible says we are "conformed to the image of his son." We end up looking more like Jesus, and that makes the Father happy.

The original temptation is to try to achieve happiness through anything other than a relationship with the Father. It never works. Nothing apart from him ever satisfies. Ironically, when we instead focus solely on the happiness of the Father, we, in turn, find happiness ourselves. We can find happiness! But it is only found when we focus on the happiness of the Father. He, in turn, gives happiness to us.

The Happiness of God

What if the only thing that mattered to the Father was his desire to spend time with you? What if he only cared about that? What if dwelling with his kids was the singular thing that made him happy? What if he didn't care if you had an affair? What if he didn't care if you were addicted to porn, alcohol, prescription drugs, or meth? What if he didn't care if you were greedy? What if he didn't care if you were gay or straight? What if he didn't care if you were filled with pride? What if he didn't care if you served him? What if none of those things mattered to God, and the only thing he wanted was to be with you, to have an intimate, personal relationship with you? Would that change the way you view God?

Imagine a father whose child is lost. He frantically searches for the child, desperate to reconnect with him. He doesn't care if the child has willfully wandered away. He only wants to have the child safely back in his arms. It is all he cares about at that moment. He can address any other issues later. Right now, at this moment, the only thing that matters is restoration. This is how the Father God sees us.

We tend to believe we must fix ourselves up to come to the Father, but nothing could be further from the truth. It is when we come to him, in all our glorious mess, we find him reaching down to us, pulling us onto his lap. In his love, he transforms our chaos into something of beauty. He doesn't leave us in the state we are when we come to him. No, he changes us. He washes us with his love. He brushes the dirt from our faces. He licks his finger and wipes the smudge from our cheek. He transforms us at the deepest places in our lives. He does this because it makes him happy to change us. It is always about his happiness.

Our understanding of the Father's desire to dwell with us begins in the Garden. Scroll back to the beginning of creation. God creates a perfect earth and places a man and a woman within a special garden called Eden. Remember, the Bible says the Father would walk with Adam and Eve in the cool of the evening. Imagine the time they spent together. They had no needs. They likely spent their time together enjoying one another's companionship. The love they experienced as they walked together was profound. For God is love, and to be in his presence is to experience his love to the full. There was no emptiness in their lives. There was no striving to fill a void. All was perfect and in order. The Father was happy.

Sin came and ruined it all. And so it was the Father sent his son from the splendor of heaven to pay the penalty for our sin. Again, heaven held its breath. A tiny, fragile baby born to a teenage mother cried out from a rented room. The plan had begun. From those humble beginnings, the Son of God walked our dusty planet, endured the abuse of a sin-cursed world, and eventually gave his life to pay the penalty for our sin. Someone had to die. The sacrifice had to be perfect. Spotless. Pure.

The world held its breath for three days. Then, in an earthquake that shook the heavens, Jesus rose from the dead. He cast aside the bonds of earth and returned to the Father. Again, the importance of this moment in history is hard to overstate. Because now, the Father could reconnect with his kids. The payment for sin was paid in full. All of heaven rejoiced! The Father could be happy again.

When you and I understand the depth of the transaction made on our behalf, we can be restored in relationship with the

Father. The father-child relationship is what makes him happy. We come to him with all our faults and failures. He does not ask us to fix ourselves before we come to him. Because the perfect one paid the penalty for us, the Father accepts us just as we are. Because his son was perfect, we do not have to be perfect ourselves. This is why the Father does not care if we had an affair. He doesn't care if we are addicted to porn, alcohol, prescription drugs, or meth. He doesn't care if we are greedy. He does not care if we are gay or straight. He doesn't care if we serve him. At this moment, he only cares that we accept the gift he offers us on our behalf. He only cares that he might be able to dwell with us again. So deep is his love for us. In time, his love transforms our lives. Issues that seemed impossible to overcome melt in the presence of pure love. His love reforms us into beautiful creatures. What matters at this moment is that we accept the gift of forgiveness he gives us.

If the Father God's desire is to dwell with us, then what would happen if we made it our focus to dwell with him? What if we spent our days with him as we work, shuttling kids to school, cleaning the house, working in the yard, etc. Our focus becomes dwelling with him in every aspect of our lives. We are his children, living with the Father through this life in our house until one day we get to live with him, face to face in his house. Dwelling with us is what makes the Father happy. And this is where our happiness begins.

The Pursuit of Happiness

In 1776, the writers of the Declaration of Independence inscribed a phrase into the vernacular of the American mindset that has done more harm than any other ideal declared in this document. It was the declaration that we had the right to "life, liberty, and the pursuit of happiness." From this moment forward, we lost our way. Ironically, the writers of the Declaration of Independence only gave us the right to pursue happiness. They never guaranteed we would grasp it. All we found was a ragged pursuit that left us empty in the end.

The American Dream says we will be happy when we are successful. We will be happy when we are in a relationship. We will be happy if we make more money per hour. We will be happy if we live in a better neighborhood. We will be happy if we lose weight. We will be happy if we upgrade. And on it goes. Yet, we are never happy. We try all these things, only to find we are not any happier than when we started. Something is amiss.

Humanism, in broad strokes, is the idea that the end of all things is the happiness of man. On the surface, this sounds attractive. It is the American way. And it is built into the idea of the American Dream. If we work hard, study long, and dream big, eventually, we will snatch the golden ticket. Countless online videos tell us to pursue our dreams. Most self-help books fall into this category. You can help yourself! You have everything you need within you to succeed! Much of contemporary ministry in our churches in North America falls into this category. Often the message is focused on helping people to be happier in their lives. Message series are based on felt needs and what the Bible says about them. On the surface, it sounds good. But a closer look reveals a root of humanism spreading through contemporary churches.

I have lost count of the number of self-help books I have read through the years. When I felt room for improvement, I created goals and then made lists to break down how I would achieve those goals. It was a lot of work, but I was pursuing my dreams! I lived a life most people could only imagine. I built a career that allowed me to travel the world. I once sat beside a bonfire in Africa, watching tribesmen dance for a wedding that was taking place in the morning. I witnessed a cheetah attack on a herd of gazelle while on safari in Kenya. I slept on the open plains in central Africa. I backpacked across Europe, went skiing in the Alps, drank wine in France, and ate gelato in Italy. I visited art museums and botanical gardens on several continents. I ate fried calamari from street vendors in China. I felt the warmth of the sun on my skin on a rock-strewn beach in Croatia. I ate seafood on both coasts of Canada and tented my way across Alaska. Closer to home, I wrote music and found success on the radio. I visited every state in the Union. I bought and sold homes, profiting along the way. I lived on a sailboat for four years. I was on a major American TV game show and won $20,000.

I pursued anything that seemed interesting. And none of it made me happy. None. None of it lasted. None of it was wrong; it just failed to provide happiness. There was nothing wrong with doing those things. But, in the end, I was no happier than when I began. Each moment brought a temporary high, but it never lasted. I traveled the world but never punched the golden ticket.

Herein lies the problem. We unknowingly follow a humanistic mindset as we navigate our lives. We chase happiness. We even tend to drag this philosophy into our Christian experience. We believe God wants us to be happy. So our prayers focus on what would make us happy if only God were to answer our prayers. We write lists of things to pray for, hoping God will answer our prayers. Why? Because we think it would make us happy if things turned out the way we pray.

I lived this way for most of my life. Then I started questioning the idea of living for my happiness. I could not find anywhere in the Bible where the focus was my happiness. The Bible seemed to be about the happiness of God. The story of a father who wants to dwell with his kids appeared preeminent from beginning to end. This caused a fundamental shift in my thinking. What if, instead of focusing on my happiness, I focused on the happiness of God? How would my life look? What makes him happy? What does the Father God want?

Suddenly, I saw my life from a new perspective. For once, the focus of my life would be the happiness of the Father. The idea rushed through my veins like an electrical surge. What if I ordered my life around anything that made him happy? What would please him today? It seemed too simple. It felt revolutionary.

What if I set aside everything I thought I knew and simply spent time on his lap?

There was a sense of still yearning for more. It was like I had all this success and it was still like: I'm still sad, and I'm still in pain. And I still have these unresolved issues. And I thought all the success was going to make everything good. And so for me, the drugs were a numbing agent to just continue to get through. And then you wake up one day... and you're unhappy and you have all this success in the world, but you're just like: Well, what is this worth if I'm still feeling empty inside?

—Justin Bieber
Singer

Chapter 5

Separated from the Father

My journey into this relationship with the Father began with a single question. Why did God choose the term "Father" to describe himself? It seemed odd to me. He could have chosen any word. He could have called himself "The All-Powerful One" to remind us he could squash us like a bug with the tip of his finger. He could have called himself "The All-Knowing One" and remind us he knows everything we have done wrong. He could have called himself "The Most-High-All-Present God" and remind us he is present everywhere, watching, judging, condemning. He could have used any number of different names, but he chose the word "Father." Why the name "Father"?

I searched the Old Testament in the Bible, expecting to find references to him as a father throughout the stories of creation, the flood, the line of Abraham, Moses, and David. I thought I would see him as a father within the pages of the Psalms, the prophets, or the historical stories. Instead, what I found was only eight references to God as Father in the entire Old Testament. Only eight. Eight references throughout thirty-nine books. Eight references in historical passages covering around four thousand years of history. Eight uses in 582,100 words in the English translation. Eight. I was stunned. I sat staring at my laptop, dumbfounded by the revelation.

So I turned to the New Testament. What I discovered further confounded me. In John's account of the story of the birth, life, and death of Jesus, there are 117 references to God as a father! One hundred seventeen references in one book alone. Again, only eight references in the entire Old Testament. I felt I had discovered a long-buried treasure. The more I searched, the more I uncovered. Now, I stood back and surveyed what I had found.

From the moment Jesus began his public ministry, he was trying to introduce us to the Father. Over and over, he spoke of the Father in intimate terms. Again and again, he invited us to know the Father. How had I missed this? How, in over fifty years of attending church, had I not been introduced to the Father? Jesus I knew. The Holy Spirit I knew. But the Father remained a shadowy figure out of focus in the background of the photo of the Trinity. When I was a child attending Sunday school, I sang, "Jesus loves me, this I know...." We never sang, "The Father loves me, this I know for the Bible tells me so." I only knew the Father as the one who could squash me. I feared the Father. In my mind, he was the God of the Old Testament, the God of Abraham, Isaac, and Moses, the All-Powerful One, the one you approached with trembling knees and downcast eyes if you dared to approach him at all. I served him, but I couldn't say I loved him. I obeyed him because I feared the repercussions if I didn't. I had an affinity for him, but to say I loved him with all of my heart was not my reality.

I began a quest to learn more about this Father who wanted to dwell with me. What if the Father God truly wanted an intimate relationship with me? How would that relationship look?

Slowly, cautiously, I began to seek him. If the heart of the Father God was to dwell with his kids, what if I made the focus of my life to dwell with him?

I thought obedience was the only thing that mattered. Just follow the rules, and everything will work out well. I was a model Christian, but did I have a relationship with the Father? Not much anyway.

For years I muddled along, trying to live the best I could, always yearning for more. On the outside, my life looked successful. I had a promising career. I traveled extensively for work and pleasure. I sought adventure, checking boxes on my bucket list along the way. But always, I felt empty inside. Something was still out of line. The Father-shaped hole remained, longing to be filled.

Separated from the Father

Most of the time, I think my sin is no big deal. Most of the time, my sin has little consequence. At least that is what I used to think. Now I see it differently. Now I understand my sin separates me from the Father God.

Remember, we inherently know when we have sinned. You know it as well as I do. God wired the code into our DNA. From birth, we instinctively know when we do something wrong. We hide the evidence. We witness this behavior when a young child snatches away a toy from another and then tries to hide the behavior. We try to convince ourselves our behavior is not that bad. But we know it is wrong. I don't have to give you a list. You already have the list within you. Our conscience shares the list with us. It may speak quietly at first, but eventually, it shouts. Sometimes we try to silence its voice, but always it reappears, in the background, pricking at our mind like a mosquito. We swat it away while we continue our behavior. But inherently, we know when we are wrong.

I used to think my sin was no big deal because I used the Father's willingness to forgive as a get out of jail free card. When I considered looking at porn online, I knew I could ask the Father God to forgive me, and he would. So I kept short accounts with him. When I failed, I was quick to seek forgiveness. But I treated sin as shallow, something normal and easily accounted for with the forgiveness of the Father.

The problem is I was seeking forgiveness without repentance. Repentance implies turning in the opposite direction.

Sin matters for one fundamental reason: because sin separates the Father from his kids. But while sin separates the Father from us, it never separates us from his love. He never stops loving us, even when sin separates us from him. While we are sinning, he aches to reconnect with us. Across the universe, he calls to us, drawing us to himself. He is love in its purest form. We are loved by him, even when we are separated from him by sin. He loves the one who doesn't believe he exists just as much as he loves the one who has committed his life to him. If you have human DNA, you are loved. Period. End of sentence. So while sin severs the relationship, it never separates us from his love for us.

Yes, the Father hates sin. Why shouldn't he? You would hate it too if it separated you from your children. You would long to hold your kids in your arms. You would do anything to restore the relationship. You would never stop loving them. You would find a way to have them back on your lap, safe in your embrace, which is precisely what the Father does for us.

Our enemy knows that sin separates the Father from his kids. Sometimes I think he understands this better than we do. For as much as the Father is love, our enemy is hate. He hates the Father. He wants nothing less than to stick it in the eye of the Father and keep him separated from us. You and I are collateral damage in his war with the Father God. Our enemy wants us to believe our sin is of little consequence. "It's not that bad," he whispers. We tend to agree.

But because the Father is perfectly holy, our sin separates him from us. Even at the cross, when Jesus was dying to pay the penalty for our sins, the Father God could not look on his own Son. Jesus took our sin upon him, and for a brutal moment, the Father had to look away. At that moment, Jesus felt what we feel today. Because he bore our sin, it separated him from his Father. In sadness, he cries, "My God, my God, why have you forsaken me." At that moment, he does not care that his body is wrecked, soaked in blood, pain surging through him like electricity. He cares that our sin has separated him from the Father.

Reconnecting with the Father

The good news is that when we understand how sin separates us from the Father, we can take strides toward restoring the relationship with him. We marvel at the price Jesus paid on our behalf. We find forgiveness we did not deserve. It is when we do not understand this simple truth that we stay stuck where we are. Please don't shy away from dealing with sin. It is the first of many steps toward healing.

Reading this now, at this stage of our journey to the lap of God, you may find it difficult to imagine your sin is a big deal. But once we have experienced the love of the Father, we are never the same. The thought of being separated from him wrecks us. And suddenly, what seemed small and insignificant, now matters greatly.

Alone, in the quiet of the morning, I sat in my favorite chair, pondering this thought. How is it God created *me* to have a relationship with him? How could it be the Father God wanted to dwell with me? Me, the kid with all the problems. Me, the one who had made such a mess of my life.

A cup of coffee sat beside me on the end table, steaming, inviting. On the other side of the table was a matching, empty chair. I looked at the chair, imagining the Father God sitting beside me, and began to talk with him, eyes open, halting voice.

"Father," I said, "I don't know what I am doing. But it seems like you want to be a father to me. If that is true, I need you to help me to understand this."

Silence. There was no audible reply from the chair beside me. The heavens didn't open. There was no shaft of golden light illuminating the room, no sound of angel wings rustling in the air. But in that quiet moment, a relationship of love with the Father was born.

My life would never be the same.

*Truly I tell you, anyone who will
not receive the kingdom of God like a
little child will never enter it.*

—*Jesus*

Chapter 6

Becoming a Child Again

As I began to view my life and relationship with the Father God through the lens of his happiness, I pondered what my life would look like in that kind of relationship. For most of my life, my goal was to learn more Bible knowledge, to understand deep areas of theology, to mature and grow in my relationship with God. I saw myself as growing up into adulthood. But now, I questioned this approach. Perhaps my focus had been wrong. The more I understood what it meant to be in a relationship with the Father God, the more I saw myself as a toddler on his lap. I was learning to be a child again. What if I focused on being a kid again, growing younger instead of older, a sort of Benjamin Button Christianity?

Again, I turned to the Bible to see what it said.

From the infant born in a stable in Bethlehem, Jesus grew into a young man. Finally, in his early thirties, he began revealing the purpose for why he came. Little by little, he shared the secret of his relationship with the Father. Astonishing miracles bore witness to his authority. Crowds grew larger with each miraculous event. His fame spread like wildfire on the Galilean hills.

As Jesus' persona grew in celebrity, his closest followers, the disciples, acted as a sort of gatekeeper. Imagine the bodyguards surrounding the Pope when he visits a country, and it will give you an idea of what it was like for Jesus. When the Pope arrives, paparazzi surge forward to catch a photo of the moment. As he walks along the rope-line, a sea of people hold out cell phones, cameras rolling, hoping for a video to share on social media. Mothers hold out their babies, longing for a blessing.

Now imagine Jesus in the scene. A crush of people followed him everywhere, eager to see a miracle, vying for a glimpse of the prophet. Then, like the Pope, people brought children to Jesus, hoping he would touch the infants and bless them. The disciples, well-intentioned, tried to stop it. "Leave Jesus alone," they said, blocking the parents from bringing their babies to him. But when Jesus saw what was happening, he was appalled. "What are you doing? Please don't stop the children from coming to me. Bring them! The kingdom of God belongs to kids. In fact, if you don't receive the kingdom of God like a little child, you'll never enter it." The disciples looked at each other, unsure how to proceed.

Then Jesus edged past the disciples and picked up a little girl, sweeping her into his embrace, kissing her face. The child giggled and shyly turned her head away. Jesus brushed the hair from her eyes so he could see her beautiful face. She blushed. He smiled as he placed his hand on her head and blessed her.

Pause for a minute and let this image sink into your mind. In this story from the Bible, Jesus, the Son of God, holds a child in his embrace. He steps past the gatekeepers and models the relationship of a child with her father. Coming as a little child, he says, is what it takes to be part of the family of God. This is how we enter the kingdom of God. We must come as a child. There is no other way. This childlike attitude is where it all begins. Everything else depends on this one thing. How can this be? Then it occurred to me. The Father cannot father us if we are not children.

Embracing Childhood

How had I missed this? Somehow, we missed the relationship with the Father. Instead, we focused on following rules, liturgy, church attendance, and service order. Religion, the one thing intended to show us the way to God, had become the gatekeeper, stiff-arming us from approaching the Father, keeping us at a distance from him.

What if, instead of focusing on being religious, we made it our goal to become children again? What if we saw ourselves as children, embraced by the Father?

You long to be held by the Father, to feel his kiss on your cheek. He edges past the religious leaders and sweeps you up into his arms. You turn your head shyly away, only to find him brushing the hair from your eyes so he can see your beautiful face. Ah, but then he places his hand on your head. Softly he whispers a blessing to you so profound, so beautiful, so loving. You are speechless at the moment, and you will never be the same.

The fundamental element necessary to be in the family of God is to be a child. Again, the Father cannot father us unless we are children. We view everything else that follows through the lens of a father and a child. Obeying what the Father tells us to do is viewed through this lens. Maturing in our relationship with the Father is viewed through this lens. Helping others into the family is seen through this perspective. Everything that follows depends on our understanding of the roles of a father and child.

Giving Up Trying to Be a Good Christian

Traditionally our approach to being a good Christian involves setting a series of goals to discipline ourselves to become the model Christian. For example, we set a goal to attend church every Sunday. Next, we set a goal to read the Bible every day. Then we set a goal to spend a certain amount of time in prayer every day. We set a lot of goals.

What usually happens is we see success for a few weeks. At first, our newly found success feels liberating. We celebrate the achievement of the goal! Then, a few weeks later, we are right back where we began. The problem is that although we achieved the goal, we haven't experienced transformation. We check off the box, draw a line through an item on a list, but achieving the goal has not transformed us. We need transformation, not momentary success. Transformation comes when we become a child of the Father, spending time with him in his embrace, filled to the full with his love. Out of that relationship, he utterly transforms our lives. This is the transforming power of being a child on his lap.

Before I understood that coming to the Father as a child is what matters, I spent years trying to be a good Christian, failing miserably along the way. I worked hard to follow the rules. The model was perfection, and I could never quite reach it. So I was always striving, working, exhausting myself. I wore myself out traveling, speaking in churches and conferences, schlepping through airports and hotel breakfast buffets. I was home on average around ten days a month. I was serving God! I thought that was what was important.

Behind the scenes, I was empty. No matter how many times I set a goal to be holy and pure, I still fell back into old patterns with pornography. Failure frustrated me immensely. I cycled through repenting, living a clean life, feeling tempted, and falling into old habits before repenting and starting the cycle over again. Sound familiar? Insert your particular issue here. We want to live rightly before God. We genuinely try. But we fail because our focus is on the wrong area. We are focusing on completing goals. We should focus on becoming a child in love with the Father. We should focus on becoming the kind of people who have a deep, loving relationship with the Father. We should become children in his arms, whole, secure, filled to the full with his love, with little room for thoughts of disobedience.

The irony is when our focus is on holiness and purity, there is little thought of the relationship with the Father. Our focus is on ourselves and how we need to be better. But when our focus is on the relationship with the Father, there is little thought of holiness and purity because obedience naturally flows from the relationship. So when I am feeling tempted with pornography, the problem is not the temptation; the issue is that there is a breakdown in my relationship with the Father. I need to sit on his lap for a while and reconnect with him. The time I spend with him affects every aspect of my life.

This principle transforms every area of our lives. Time spent with the Father affects everything! Better to become a child of the Father. My focus is on becoming the kind of person who has a childlike relationship with the Father. How does that kind of person live? What if I focused on becoming that child instead of focusing on a series of goals?

Further, toddlers don't set goals. Toddlers just love being held. A toddler doesn't come to his father with a list of things he needs. The child's father already knows what the child needs. The child just wants to spend time with his father, to be held in his embrace. What if we had that kind of relationship with the Father God? What if his embrace satisfied us fully?

Traditionally, our focus is to discipline ourselves to achieve a high standard of what we believe a good Christian is. But in the father and child model, our focus is simply on dwelling with the Father.

Giving Up Trying to Serve God

Sometimes I feel like I am trying to unwind generations of programming that told me what I do for God is what matters. If what we do for God is the highest thing, then we serve a twisted Father.

The Bible says the most important command is to love the Father with all our hearts, all our minds, all our strength. The command is not to serve him with all our hearts; it is to love him with all our hearts. All. Not just saying I love him but loving him in such a way that nothing else matters.

Often, we are concerned with discerning what God wants us to do for him. We say we are trying to find God's will for our lives. But the Father has already told us what he wants us to do. He wants us to love him with all our hearts. When we do this, then out of the relationship with him, we discover many beautiful ways to serve him. We serve him because we love him! This makes all the difference. Instead, we try to serve him without a relationship with him, and it only leads to burnout, weariness, following rules, going to church, going through the motions, looking on the outside like a religious person but with no relationship with the Father. When finally, we are confronted with our lack of relationship, we are appalled. And what is our response? We try to discipline ourselves to get back to where we think we need to be instead of setting all our efforts aside and learning to be still on his lap.

The Bible says "the gate is wide and the way is easy that leads to destruction, and those who enter by it are many. For the gate is narrow and the way is hard that leads to life, and those who find it are few." I can't help but wonder if Jesus was speaking this in context with the understanding that I must come as a child to enter the kingdom of God. What if the broad path led to sitting in a pew, going through the motions of being religious, working harder and harder to achieve some standard, and the narrow path was simply coming as a child and sitting on the lap of God? It is something to consider.

Consider also how Jesus referred to himself as the Son of God. He could have chosen any term to describe our relationship with God. Just as he chose the word "Father" to describe God, he also chose the word "Son" to describe himself. He could have called himself the "Servant sent from God Almighty, the most high God". Then he could invite all of us to join him as servants of God. Practically speaking, that is what most of us believe. We see ourselves as servants to God, wondering aloud what he would have us to do for him. But Jesus doesn't define us as servants. No! He invites us to join him in the family. He welcomes us as adopted siblings with all the rights and privileges of a natural-born child. He even describes the process of adoption as being born again, born of spirit into the spiritual relationship with the Father.

My friend, we must be born again. For the Father cannot father us until we come as a child.

Everyone who drinks of this water will be thirsty again, but whoever drinks of the water that I will give him will never be thirsty again.

—*Jesus*

Chapter 7

Conversations with the Father

I grew in my childlike relationship with the Father. Where earlier I had sat in a chair and imagined the Father sitting next to me, now I began to see myself as a child on his lap. In my mind, I saw myself as a toddler. I would crawl over to him, and he would reach down and pull me onto his lap. Sitting there with him, leaning back into his chest, I would speak with him about issues concerning me, thoughts from my day, some random thought of nothing of importance. The conversations that followed were intimate, deeply personal. Sometimes I cried with him over something that had happened to me. Sometimes I laughed with him over some silly moment that occurred at the grocery store. Sometimes I sat in silence, just needing to be held. I began to understand what it meant to pray without words.

For most of my life, I followed the rules of what a good Christian does. Built into that expectation is the importance of prayer. As a child, I remember visiting speakers teaching about prayer. It always involved some sort of formula. Usually, there was some sort of list.

Like most good Christians, I was taught to pray with some sort of structure, a way to organize my prayers so I would miss nothing. We used formulas to arrange our prayers. One traveling minister taught our congregation how to pray all night. He even had a pie chart showing the time we needed to spend in various categories. This guy raised the bar. How spiritual you must be to be able to do that.

In my college years, I attended a Christian university. A particularly zealous roommate set his alarm for an ungodly hour to rise from slumber and kneel beside his bed in prayer. His alarm always woke me up, disrupting my sleep. Hours later, when my alarm finally went off, I would find him still kneeling beside his bed, head in his hands, firmly asleep. Someone taught him a particular time of prayer was more godly than another.

Now I began to question my own time in prayer with the Father. How did Jesus speak with his Father? In the quiet moments alone, away from the crush of the crowds, how did he pray? Do you think he used a list? Do you think he spent this precious time with his Father reading aloud a list of things he needed? I cannot even imagine this. Or when Adam and Eve spent time with the Father in the Garden of Eden, how did they speak with the Father? Again, do you think they had a list? Did they meet with the Father in the cool of the evening, sitting together beneath the spreading branches of a tree, and pull out a list of things and people they were praying for? They had no needs. So we can erase that section off the list. What was left? What is left on our prayer lists if we remove needs? Anything? In the context of a relationship, does any of this make sense?

Why God Created Prayer

Looking at the example of Adam and Eve in the garden made me question my own time spent with the Father. If I were meeting with the Father in a beautiful garden, what would we talk about? What would that conversation look like? Adam and Eve had a perfect relationship with the Father God. They had no needs. Needs would come later, after the fall, after sin entered the relationship.

I pondered the conversations they had with the Father. But remember, sin entered the picture, and sin separates! The Father could no longer spend time lounging with his kids. Sin cast Adam and Eve out of the perfect garden and out of the perfect union with the Father. What was the Father to do? He still longed for the time he spent with his kids. His heart ached to be able to speak with them. And then it hit me. What if the Father God created prayer so he would have a way to stay connected with his kids until he was finally reunited with them again?

I turned to the pages of the Bible, searching for any mention of prayer before the moment of sin. None. Not a single mention. In fact, the first mention of prayer comes much, much later. Adam and Eve did not need prayer before the fall. They spoke face to face with the Father. In the future, prayer will not be needed when the Father dwells with us in the new heaven and earth. Again, we will speak with him face to face. Prayer, it would seem, is for the in-between. It is a way for the Father to stay connected with his kids until finally he is reunited with them.

Prayer is for the happiness of the Father. And once we understand prayer is for the happiness of the Father, it changes everything. It changes the way we speak with him, how often we speak with him throughout the day, and what we talk about with him.

The Parable of the Father and the Phone

Once upon a time, there was a father who had a lovely daughter. She was his pride and joy. Oh, how he loved her. He relished the time they spent together. Her laughter filled his heart to overflowing. The daughter grew and, finally, the dreaded day came when she was leaving for college. His heart ached at the thought of her moving so far from his embrace. But he had a plan. He bought her the best cell phone he could afford. He paid for the monthly service so it would be no expense for her. He imagined the conversations they would have. He looked forward to hearing every detail of her day. He could hardly wait. With a twinkle in his eye, he surprised her with the gift. He beamed when he saw her face light up with the discovery.

They said their goodbyes, clinging to one another one last time, hiding their tears from the other. The ache in the father's heart grew stronger as he watched the car pull away, move down the street, and turn the corner until, at last, he lost the car from view. The separation was dreadful. But, he reminded himself, she had the phone. They would speak soon.

And so he waited for her call. When she finally called, it was brief. She was on her way to class, no time to talk, but she needed more money transferred to her account. He was delighted to hear her voice and thrilled to meet the need. But the call left him unsettled. He was hoping for a conversation. He longed to know how she was adapting to her new environment. What were her roommates like? Was she alright? Oh, how he longed to hear her laugh. Oh, how he longed to hear her rambling on about nothing of importance as they used to do at home.

In time, it only grew worse. At some point, the father realized the only time she called was when she needed something. He had bought the cell phone for her, hoping they could stay connected. He had paid the price for the monthly plan. But the only time she used it was when she needed something. The realization broke him at a place he had not felt before.

My friend, the Father God created prayer so he could stay connected with us until we are finally back home with him. He paid the price for this privilege by giving his own Son to die for us. And then the only time we use this privilege is when we need something. The realization breaks the heart of the Father God. This is not what he intended.

Further, when we spend time in conversation with someone, there is always a back and forth. We speak for a moment, then the other chimes in. That's the nature of a conversation. When we understand prayer as a conversation with the Father, it changes how we spend prayer time with him. At some point, we learn to listen. What does the Father want to say? What about his part of the conversation?

The Parable of the Awkward Conversation

Imagine a newlywed husband and wife. They are in the throes of love. He writes a beautiful letter to her, sharing his profound love for her. With pride, he gives her the letter. To his delight, the letter is a treasure to her. She reads every line, every nuance, drinking deeply of his affection. To be loved so fully is a dream. To his surprise, she suggests they spend time together every morning. At this, his heart leaps. Nothing would thrill him more than to spend that time with her. Throughout their busy days, they will reconnect with a text or a call. But those moments in the morning will be a treasure for him.

They sit together on the couch while the sun is still below the horizon, long before the press of responsibilities of the day collide. To his delight, she takes his letter and begins to read. He watches the look on her face as she reads of his love for her.

Then, she sits the letter aside. He can tell she is pondering the words he has written. He waits in anticipation to see how she will respond. What will they talk about today, he wonders. He can hardly wait to see how the conversation will progress.

But as he sits there quietly, a strange thing happens. She reaches for a sheet of paper upon which she has written a few items she needs his help with that day. Odd, he thinks to himself. But he allows her to continue. She reads the list to him. He nods as she progresses down the list. One by one, he considers each request and mentally confirms he is able to do each one. Finally, she finishes the list. Then, to his dismay, she sits the list aside, thanking him for helping her, and rises and leaves to go and get ready for work.

He sits there in shock as the scent of her perfume leaves the room. What just happened? She had read the letter. She had pondered what it said. She had shared a list of things she needed and even thanked him for his help. But not once had she given him an opportunity to speak. Not once. The realization that their expectations of the time together were dramatically different cut him deeply. He sat there reeling from the observation. He had expected that they would have a deep conversation, perhaps sharing their love for one another. He thought he would have a moment when he could tell her how much he adored her, how the way she walked through a room lit a fire within him, how he treasured her. But she gave him no place, no opportunity to do so.

The realization took his breath away. He wondered how long they could last if this were the pattern of their relationship.

My friend, our Father longs to sit with us, to have a conversation with us, to tell us how much he loves us. For our part, we read the Bible, his love letter to us, and ponder who he is and how he loves us. Then we set it aside, pick up a list, and read to him everything we need for the day. Finished, we fold up the list and go about our day until the next morning when we settle in again to repeat the scenario. In Christian circles, we call this "having devotions." But is this actually what the Father wanted? Is this why he sent his Son to die for us? Does he sit in silence beside us, waiting for his moment to speak, but we are so preoccupied with our list that we ignore him? What would he want to say? Would he love to tell us how much he loves us, how he aches to be with us, how he longs for the day when we will finally be home with him? And are we missing all of it because we have not learned to listen to his voice?

Furthermore, what does it say about our relationship with him if we feel we need to discipline ourselves to spend time with him? Again, if I am married and I tell my wife we need to discipline ourselves to spend time together, what does that say about our relationship? And if the time together is so boring and I can hardly keep my attention on the other person, what does that say? Is this even close to what the Father intended? As I looked into the Bible, I found no example of this kind of relationship with the Father. Yes, bring your requests to him. Yes, give thanks for his provision and kindness. Yes, do all this, but always in the context of relationship. And always be ready to listen.

I decided to reassess the time I spent with the Father. What if I focused my relationship with him in conversation as if we were together in the Garden of Eden? How would that relationship look? How would my discussion with him sound? Would I have a list of needs I needed him to take care of, or would my time with him be a natural back and forth, speaking, listening, enjoying the companionship? I opted for the latter.

So now we sit together and share with one another. Often, I am the one sitting in silence, listening in my mind to the voice of the Father telling me how much he loves me. Those moments are a treasure.

Instead of focusing on reading a certain number of chapters in the Bible each day, then praying through a list, I sit with the Father and have a conversation with him. I speak with him about anything that comes to mind. Each day is different with no agenda. Sometimes there are pressing needs, and we talk each one through, gaining his perspective, his wisdom for each situation. Sometimes he brings a passage from the Bible to mind, and I read it to learn what he is trying to say to me. Sometimes he brings a worship song to mind, and I play it on my phone, listening intently to hear what he is saying to me. Most times, we just speak of our love for one another. When I am speaking, much of the time, I am simply telling him how much I love him, how I long to be with him, how nothing in this world feels attractive to me anymore because his love for me has filled me to the full. I want nothing but his embrace, his affection, his love pouring over me, pouring through me.

Avoiding Routine

But even in these moments set aside to reconnect with the Father, I find myself going through the motions. I tend to fill my prayers with cliches. I caught myself doing it one morning as I sat spending some time with the Father before beginning to write. "Father," I said, "I bow before you this morning...." I stopped mid-sentence, aware that I was not thinking about what I was saying. Is it appropriate to bow before the Father? Of course! Is it right to say I am bowing before him when my mind and heart are miles away, focused on something else, with no thought of actually prostrating myself before him? Of course not! So I stopped praying and sat in stillness for a moment.

I find that sitting in silence at the beginning of a conversation with the Father, centering my thoughts on him, is one of the best ways to begin a conversation with him. I am about to have a conversation with someone I treasure, who also happens to be the King of all kings, the all-powerful one. I take a moment to process this truth to keep from babbling on with cliches.

One of the most telling commands Jesus gives in the Bible is the command not to drone on when we are praying. "When you pray," he says, "do not heap up empty phrases as the Gentiles do, for they think that they will be heard for their many words. Do not be like them, for your Father knows what you need before you ask him." We are having a conversation with him, not an interrogation or word-crafting marathon. Our Father already knows our needs. So we can keep it real when we are speaking with him.

I wondered why this was so difficult for me to do. Then I realized it was not what was modeled to me from as early as I can remember in my religious upbringing. Prayer was not personal. Reverent cliches were the norm. We addressed our prayers to the God of the Old Testament, the one who could squash you. So we believed we better use the correct language when we approached him. I do not recall hearing an intimate conversation with the Father from the pulpit in the church I attended. Reverence? Yes. Intimacy? No.

In many churches I have visited, I have witnessed this practice of filling our prayers with religious cliches. Rarely do I hear someone from the pulpit praying as if they are speaking with someone. Instead, I cringe at some of the prayers I hear. It is care-less prayer. It is a prayer spoken without care. It feels like nothing more than a transitional element in the service order. We say a prayer to start the service. Then we say a prayer at the end of worship to transition the service into the message or the offering. But are we actually speaking with the Father? It doesn't seem like it. Then we close the service with prayer. And the ones who are exceptionally good at it can pray the three points of the sermon as if somehow God needed to be reminded of the points. It is shocking how we pray in our churches today. Perhaps your church is different. I sincerely hope it is.

Further complicating our relationship with the Father, we try to replicate this model of public prayer in our personal prayer time with him. Since these kinds of careless prayers are what we see modeled from the platform in our churches, our personal prayers become filled with cliches, endless prattling on in clever religious language, with little recognition we are speaking one-on-one with the most amazing Father of all time. Jesus says, "Don't do this!"

When Jesus teaches us how to pray, he addresses God as "our Father," reminding us we are speaking as children to our Father. It is a relational conversation. We are not addressing his majesty the king, with all the pomp and circumstance associated with a royal. We are speaking with our Father!

Further, just like a toddler coming to his father, our Father already knows our needs before we ask him. So, yes, we may bring our concerns and needs to the Father. He wants us to do this! But we bring them to him as part of a conversation with him. We speak with normal, everyday language, the same language we would use if you and I were sitting together, sharing our concerns.

We come to him to spend time with him. We begin with a simple prayer.

"Father, help me to learn to listen."

The image of the father is fragmented and distributed among the community. But it's very, very difficult to not have a father.

—*Jordan Peterson*
Author, Canadian clinical psychologist

Chapter 8

Learning to Listen

My journey to understanding prayer as a conversation with the Father began unexpectedly. At the time, I followed the pattern taught to me by my religious upbringing. I practiced "having devotions." Traditionally, it is a time set aside to read the Bible or other devotional book and pray. Because I was trying to be a good Christian, my routine was to have my devotions in the morning before starting my workday.

My pattern was to rise well before sunrise and make a cup of coffee. I would settle in on the couch. I would read the Bible for an hour or more, tracking my progress, checking off boxes on my Bible reading schedule along the way. Then I would close the Bible and transition into my prayer time. I had a prayer list, a written list of people and things that concerned me. It usually took about ten minutes for me to pray down through the list. Then, I would say, "Amen," put away my list, and go about my day as usual before repeating the process the following day.

One morning, as I was praying down my list, I felt God speaking to me. "Tim," he said, "you need to become a man of prayer." You might think this was odd. After all, I was praying through my list when he said it. But I had to agree. Praying through my list for ten minutes a day hardly qualified me as a "man of prayer."

Typically, my response would have been to try to discipline myself to pray more. Normally, I would set a goal to pray five minutes longer today than I prayed yesterday. Tomorrow I would try to pray five minutes more than I prayed today. Eventually, I would be a praying machine! From experience, I knew this method would not work. I understood that I would see success for a few weeks, then eventually, I would fall back into old patterns. Change does not come from human effort. True transformation comes from the work of the Father within me.

So the next day, I got up, made the coffee, sat on the couch, read the Bible, prayed through my list, and ended with this simple little prayer: "Father, today I pray you would help me to become a man of prayer." I said, "Amen," closed my Bible and list, and went about my day. The next day, I prayed the same thing, "Father, today I pray you would help me to become a man of prayer." Day after day, I prayed this simple little prayer. Week after week, I asked the Father to transform my life in this area.

A couple of months later, I realized the Father had utterly transformed my prayer life. Over time, the Father had completely altered this aspect of my life. Where once I saw prayer through the context of a list of people and things I was praying for, now I understood prayer as a conversation with the Father. Now I experienced prayer in the context of a relationship with a living, breathing person.

As I grew in my understanding of my relationship with the Father, my times sitting and talking with him became my favorite moments of the day. The time with him felt nourishing, like salve to a wound. No longer were my prayer times part of a rigid devotional time. I found myself speaking with him throughout the day. Again and again, I returned to treasured moments with him, sitting with him or sitting on his lap. I spoke with him, not only for the privilege of being able to share my heart with someone I love but also for the astounding joy of hearing him talking back to me. "I love you so much," he would whisper. Over time I learned to recognize his voice in everyday moments. It was clear he wanted to speak with me. I only needed to learn to hear his voice.

Hearing the Voice of the Father

I owe much of my understanding of how the Father speaks to the work of Henry Blackaby, his son Richard Blackaby, and Claude King in their book *Experiencing God*. It was given to me by a friend in the fall of 1996. I devoured the text. It was the first time anyone had introduced me to the idea of an actual relationship with the Father. Until this point, my understanding of God was the God of the Old Testament, the one you obeyed, revered, feared. I had no expectation of hearing him speak personally to me. I obeyed the best I could but failed to have an understanding of a relationship with someone who loved me.

I was still healing from childhood trauma, searching for someone to love me. Upon reading this book, I was overwhelmed to learn God wanted to have a personal relationship with me. Me! The kid who was addicted to pornography. Me! The guy who failed in relationships. Me, the child living in an adult body, still longing for a father. The Father God wanted a relationship with me! This thought stunned me. Suddenly, I wanted to know this God who wanted to have this relationship with me. I was famished to learn about him. I read the Bible with abandon. Nothing else mattered. I wanted to know this God who wanted a relationship with me. During these months, I rarely watched TV, opting instead to read more of the Bible. I couldn't put it down. In the Old Testament, I learned how powerful he was. In the New Testament, I learned how he wanted intimacy with me as his child. It was the most amazing book I had ever read. Page after page, I learned more about the Father. In the following twelve months, I read the entire Bible cover-to-cover three times. I had found the Father I had always longed for, and nothing would keep me from learning more about him.

Thoughts of the Father consumed me. In time, those early moments of ecstasy deepened into a mature love. Frankly, I have never maintained the pace of reading the Bible from that year. But my relationship with him continues to grow.

According to Blackaby, the primary ways God speaks to us is "by the Holy Spirit through the Bible, prayer, circumstances, and the church to reveal himself, his purposes, and his ways." Within these basic parameters, there are many variations. The Father speaks in many unique ways. Often, the way the Father speaks to one person may vary from how he speaks to another. This is because we are created with a unique DNA by the Father, who knows us intimately. He knows the right way to speak to each one of us so we can hear his voice. But know this, he is speaking. We are only beginning to listen.

Explaining how the Father speaks to us is like trying to explain how radio waves travel invisibly through the air, are decoded, and broadcasted through a speaker. I cannot adequately describe or understand the process, but I enjoy listening to music on the radio. I know music when I hear it. It is the same with learning to hear the voice of the Father. Exactly how this happens, I cannot describe. But nothing thrills me more than to hear his voice.

For our purposes, I am focusing primarily on the way the Father speaks with us while we are in conversation with him, what we typically think of as prayer. I would refer you back to the *Experiencing God* study to learn more about other ways God speaks to us through the Bible, the church, and circumstances.

While we are sitting on his lap, usually, the Father speaks to us in a still, small voice. The "still, small voice" is an impression in our thoughts that speaks into our hearts. It is not an audible voice. This makes it all the more difficult to describe. How do we know we are hearing the voice of the Father and not some random thought we have generated apart from him? The best way I know to answer this is to reiterate the importance of the relationship with him. The relationship is the key to hearing the voice of the Father. If my biological dad called me on the phone, I would recognize his voice. We have a relationship as father and son. I have known him all my life. I do not have to see him to know his voice. He does not have to be physically in the room with me for me to know it is his voice speaking to me. I recognize his voice because I have a relationship with him. I have heard his voice for years. It is the same with the Father God. I recognize his voice because I have a relationship with him. I do not have to see him to know his voice. He does not have to be physically in the room with me to know it is his voice speaking to me. I recognize his voice because I have a relationship with him. I have heard his voice for years.

Finding Confirmation

Now, let's say I have an important decision to make. I ask the Father what I should do. I think I've heard him answer me, but I am not one hundred percent sure. In this case, I seek confirmation on what I believe he said. I'll say, "Father, I believe what you are telling me to do is this. I pray you would confirm this." Then I watch for confirmations. When the Father speaks, it never contradicts what the Bible already says. So I begin searching the Bible to see what the Father has said in the past.

Confirmation may also come from a conversation with a trusted friend or advisor. Confirmation may come through circumstances. Confirmation may come in any number of different ways. The key is watching for the confirmations. When we ask for confirmation, we immediately watch for an answer. He is speaking!

Once I was living in a rented one-bedroom trailer on Lemon Bay in Southwest Florida. I loved living there, but I felt the Father was leading me to move to Nashville, Tennessee. I did not want to move. I was living my beach bum fantasy life. It didn't make sense to leave paradise for Tennessee. So I prayed that if he were leading me to move, he would confirm it for me. Over the next few weeks, I listened for his voice. One morning as I sat talking with him, I said, "Father, I believe you are leading me to move, but to be honest, I'm afraid to do that." Then, that morning, while reading the Bible, I read a passage where Abraham was wrestling with God over moving to Egypt. The Bible says God replied, "Do not be afraid to go down to Egypt, for I will make you into a great nation there. I will go down to Egypt with you, and I will surely bring you back again." I had just told God I was afraid to pack up and move. Then, while reading the Bible, he shows me a story of someone else in a similar circumstance. Ah, the Father is speaking! He said to me, "Tim, I understand. You are not the first one to be afraid of following my voice. Do not be afraid. I will go with you, and I will bring you back again." He confirmed through the Bible what I had heard in a still, small voice.

During this period, the Father confirmed my move at least twenty-three times. I heard pastors on the radio address my concern. Seemingly random circumstances confirmed the move. I sought counsel from friends who confirmed God was leading me to move. Finally, one night I thought to myself, "Tim, how many confirmations is it going to take before you say the words, 'I'm moving to Tennessee.'"

The next morning, I called my friends and told them I was moving.

The Father longs to speak with us. He made a way for us to spend time with him, having a conversation with him, enjoying his presence, being washed in his love. More specifically, the Father longs to speak with you. Yes, you! He longs for you to join him on his lap, to rest there in his presence. He longs to whisper into your ear. He knows exactly how to speak with you so you will hear his voice.

Yes, the Father is still speaking. We are only beginning to learn to listen.

And so, this morning, I sat in my favorite chair in the quiet. The rising sun was sneaking through the blinds, casting long slanted shadows across the floor. I drew a long breath and slowly exhaled. I closed my eyes and saw myself tugging at the pant leg of the Father. He stopped what he was doing and reached down, sweeping me up onto his lap. I looked up into his face. He smiled, having me near. We sat in a hush for a few moments, neither of us speaking. Then, finally, I broke the silence.

"Father," I said as a smile creased my face, "I love you."

What he said next made all the difference.

I have called you by name, you are mine.

—The Father God

Chapter 9

Taking Back Our Identity

When I was in high school, I had a low view of myself. I walked this strange slackline between being in the popular group yet feeling like I didn't belong. I related more to the unpopular crowd, the lower-class crew, the ones who spent their lunch hour in the baseball dugout smoking cigarettes. As a senior, I was on the homecoming court but was not voted king. I felt empty inside. I had no sense of my own identity. I made up for it by making people laugh. I was the king of the cut-down. Insult-comedians like Joan Rivers enthralled me. The trashier, the better. I even colored my attacks with F-bombs when I thought it would get a better response.

As an adult, I continued to wrestle with identity. At a core level, I did not know who I was. A close friend of mine was a farmer. So I built my identity around being a farmer. I wore work boots and jeans. I volunteered my time on his farm. During harvest, I worked endless hours with him. I hauled wagon loads of corn or soybean from the fields back to the barns, where I unloaded them into the bins and kept the grain dryers going. I hauled beans to the mill with the semi. Once, I drove his vintage John Deere tractor in a community parade. On the surface, I looked like the faithful friend, the helpful one. But I had only become a caricature of a farmer. The outside lines looked like a farmer, but I was empty inside. Assuming the role and work of a farmer did not fill the void.

I repeated this caricature model of relationship over and over with other friends. In the end, all I wanted was to feel like I belonged to the brotherhood of men. I watched movies about World War II and envied the brotherhood forged in the heat of battle. I considered becoming a military chaplain. Another friend was a mechanic, so I hung out at the shop, learning what I could. Always I hoped I would belong, that something would satisfy. It never did.

Because I thought love would fill the void, often I built my identity around those I wanted to love me. Perhaps, if I could look like them and talk like them, then I could be whole like them. (The irony is I assumed everyone else was whole; I thought I was the only one who was empty.) And maybe they would love me. I never said it out loud, but that was certainly the reality. As a result, my relationships were a mess. On the surface, I looked like the most loving person, but I was only acting loving because I wanted to be loved. It was selfishness at the highest level.

I was fixated on trying to look the part. All my energy was spent on fixing up the outside, creating another caricature that imitated the original, but always leaving me empty inside. The Bible calls this "whitewashed tombs, which outwardly appear beautiful, but within are full of dead people's bones and all uncleanness." But, hey, I looked good in white.

I had lost my identity. I was lost. All was lost.

Finding Our Identity

Finding our identity is an elementary issue with which we all deal. Questioning our identity is even referred to in the Bible. Unfortunately, it is one of the key ways our enemy tries to prevent us from understanding our identity as kids of the Father God.

The enemy even tempted Jesus in this way. Before Jesus began his public ministry, the Bible says he was led into the wilderness to be tempted by the enemy. Within the story are lessons we can apply to our lives.

Jesus' stomach was collapsing upon itself, and a profound weakness consumed his core. Just standing up took effort, and if he stood too fast, he felt light-headed. For forty days, he had eaten nothing. Nothing passed his lips but water from a creek. He had been alone in the wilderness, set apart, led into solitude by the Spirit of the Father. But now, Jesus was no longer alone. Now, in this severely weakened state, he shared the uncomfortable moment with evil personified. The devil had come to visit.

"You know," the devil said, settling in beside him, "If you are the Son of God, command these stones to become hot, crusty loaves of bread. I know you are hungry. I know you want to eat. It's a normal human need." He paused for effect. "Do it," he whispered.

Jesus was, in fact, hungry. It was a legitimate need. It had been forty days since he had eaten. But the enemy was trying to get him to fill his stomach on his own, apart from his Father. He looked out into the desert and saw enough stones to feed five thousand if he chose to do the deed. But without bothering to turn his head toward his accuser, he said, "Man doesn't live by bread alone, but by every word that comes from the mouth of God."

Our story continues, but, for now, consider the enormity of

what has just happened. The Son of God, sent by the Father to restore his relationship with us, is approached by the devil. And what is the first thing our enemy says? "*If* you are the Son of God...." He questions Jesus' identity. Do not miss this. Pause for a moment to take this in. *If* – the most momentous two-letter word in the entire English language. Our enemy is questioning Jesus' identity as the Son of God!

We tend to read the story and gloss right over the opening statement, but it is significant our enemy begins this way. It is so significant that, when the story resumes, the devil uses the same line of attack again. This time he takes Jesus to the holy city and sets him on the pinnacle of the temple.

"If you are the Son of God," the devil continued, "throw yourself down. I mean, isn't it written that God will command his angels to take care of you? Doesn't it say they will bear you up in their hands lest you strike your foot against a stone? Come on, prove it. Jump."

"Again, it is written," Jesus replied, "'You must not put the Lord your God to the test.'"

Undeterred, the great accuser took Jesus to a high mountain and showed him all the kingdoms of the world and their glory. "See all this?" he said, sweeping his arm wide. "This is my domain. I can give it all to you. All this and more. All this glory I will give you if you only fall down and worship me."

Then Jesus said to him, "Be gone, Satan! For it is written, 'You shall worship the Lord your God, and him only shall you serve.'"

The enemy reluctantly obeyed. At last, the devil left. In his place, angels rushed in to minister to Jesus.

When I ponder this story, a singular question surfaces. Why would the enemy try to get Jesus, the Son of God, to question his identity? Twice, no less. What was I missing? Had the enemy used the same tactic with me? It would seem so.

For most of my life, I had little understanding of my identity as a son of the Father God. Lost, I floundered from relationship to relationship seeking my identity in others, only to feel exposed, threatened, ashamed, and empty. Unaware of my standing in the family of God, I sought to repair damage suffered in a chaotic childhood, hoping eventually I could find healing. Instead, my identity was for sale to the highest bidder. The one who would show me affection would win. But, oh, at such a cost.

Worse, because I tied up my identity in someone else, my worth was entirely in their hands. With my identity dependent on the other person, I could not live comfortably within my own sphere. One time, I almost got caught in my game. I called a friend. When he answered, I accidentally said, "I'm just calling to see how I'm doing today." Immediately I cringed. On the surface, it sounded like a slip of the tongue, but I knew I had just accidentally exposed my hidden agenda. I hadn't called him because I wanted to know how he was. On the contrary, I wanted to know how I was. My state of mind was entirely dependent upon his state of mind. Attaching our identity to someone else is a horrible way to live. When our identity is linked by who we are in a relationship, the other person's mindset determines our mindset. We give them complete control over our existence.

If our identity is the one who rescues, then the one in distress determines our identity. And if the person in pain finds healing, we lose our identity. Unconsciously, we may even sabotage the person from healing to maintain our identity as the healer.

If our identity is the one who is successful at work, then we give up our identity to the manager one step higher on the ladder. If the economy tanks and the company downsizes, our efforts are in vain, and our identity is lost. Some retire from a lifetime of finding identity in work and suddenly feel lost, sullen, alone. Some just keep working rather than losing their identity.

If our identity is the one who ministers, then we give up our identity to the expectations of others. Ministry needs never end. So we work day and night, sacrificing our personal lives and family at home. After all, people need us. If circumstances end a ministry career, our identity is lost. If we need a break from the pressure of ministry, our identity is lost. And on it goes.

Finding our identity in anything apart from our relationship with the Father God is not only dangerous, it also never works. It never fills the void.

Children of the Father God

However, if our sole identity is as a child of the Father God, then no one can take that from us. It is not dependent on anything we do or do not do. If we are not successful, we do not lose our identity. We are still his children even when we are having a bad day. We are his when we are tired and do not respond appropriately to wounds. We are his even when we sin. Our identity as son or daughter is not reliant on anything but our identity as his kids. The fact that the Father has adopted us gives us our identity. Finding our identity solely in our relationship with the Father frees us.

In Mark's account of the temptation of Jesus by the devil, he includes a fascinating detail leading up to the event – the baptism of Jesus. Mark shares that when Jesus was baptized, the Father says to him, "You are my beloved Son, in whom I am well pleased." The next thing that happens is the Spirit leads Jesus into the wilderness. The last thing the Father says to him before the trial is, "You are my son. I love you. You make me happy." It is as if he is intentionally reminding Jesus of the truth to carry him through the upcoming trial.

Unfortunately, our enemy would have us find our identity in anything but being a child of the Father God. Remember, our enemy is motivated by his hatred of the Father God. Because he knows it makes the Father happy to have us as his children, he will do anything to prevent the Father from having this relationship with us. He will gladly help us find our identity apart from the Father if we let him. "Just do it," he whispers. "I'll give you all this and more." But it never satisfies.

The Father of Love and the Father of Lies

Worse, often our enemy tries to get us to build our identity based on something shameful we have done. It is a hideous tactic. He labels us by our sin. He reminds us of the one time we blew it. Then, if we are not careful, we fall for it. I know I did.

Our enemy is the father of lies, and he is good at it. The key lie he tells us is that we can never change. He reminds us of a failure in our past, throwing it in our faces, dragging us back to the moment of regret. Then, at just the moment when we think we are free of it, he jerks the leash.

One day I was reading in the Bible what the apostle Paul wrote to the believers in Corinth. In this letter, he gives a laundry list of offenses that separate us from the Father: sexual immorality of all kinds, drunkenness, greed, taking advantage of others financially, and on and on. But then he states a startling fact, "And such were some of you." If we are not careful, we miss the significance of this phrase. Paul is writing to people who were following Jesus. They were part of the church that met in Corinth. Of these people, he says, some of them were formerly sexually immoral. Some were formerly alcoholics. Some were formerly greedy, and some previously took advantage of other people financially. These were the people who made up the church in Corinth. That is shocking! Paul's letter gives us great hope. We can relate to that list. I certainly do. But Paul says while this *was* our identity, *now* we are washed clean. Now we are sanctified. Now we are justified by the work of Jesus Christ on the cross and by the power of the Holy Spirit working within us. This is good news!

Our enemy wants us to create an identity based on some shameful experience in our past. He then lies and tells us we can never change. We will always be that way. That is just the way it is. Then we tell ourselves the lie, "That is just who I am. I'll never change." But when Paul says, "such were some of you," he shows us we can change. Transformation is possible! What we did in the past does not define who we are today. This is important!

Because Jesus died on the cross to pay the penalty for our sin, our identity is not based on some experience in our past. His death settled the account for our sin. His death paid it in full. Our enemy tries to form our identity based on something we did in our past. But the Father God shapes our identity based on something Jesus did in the past through his death on the cross. And what Jesus did trumps anything we did! Much as our enemy would like us to believe our past sin will always define us, that is not the case.

I released years of regret to the abyss. My failures no longer defined me. I am a son of the Father God. He loves me with all my faults and failures. He knows every sin I have ever committed and removes them from me as far as the east is from the west.

My sole identity is as a son of the Father. Period. I carefully guard this. There is constant pressure to create an identity apart from this one thing. But anytime we create an identity apart from our position as a son or daughter of God, we are in dangerous territory. Any identity we shape, apart from this intimate relationship with the Father God, can be lost. If my farmer friend retired, sold the farm, and moved to the Caribbean, I would have nothing left but a worn-out pair of jeans and work boots with dirt clods clinging to the treads. My identity would evaporate like spitting rain in a searing drought. If my identity is the one who rescues, then when the other person finds healing, I am left with nothing. There is even a temptation to define my identity as a writer or a minister. Even that is a misplaced identity. But when my identity is solely in my relationship as a son of the Father God, no one can take that identity away.

Two fathers long to give us our identity – the Father of Love and the father of lies. Which one we choose makes all the difference. The identity we accept determines the course of our lives in this world and the next. The identity that matters is the one we will have after we die. When we pass from this world to the next, if our identity is as the son or daughter of the Father God, then we spend eternity with the Father of Love. If our identity is from the father of lies, we spend eternity with him, separated forever from the Father of Love.

This is why identity matters. When we begin to understand our identity as sons and daughters of the Father, we can finally experience the fullness of his healing love. And when that happens, nothing will ever be the same.

We want people to love us, we want to be perceived well by others, or we think these material things are going to fulfill that spiritual hole we have, our emotional need. And all these drivers function on a level where we're not really aware how they are impacting our behavior and habits throughout the day.

—Rich Roll
Endurance athlete, author, podcaster

Chapter 10

Surrendering to the Father's Love

At the time, I was living in a one-bedroom trailer I rented for four hundred dollars a month. It was small and a little outdated, but it was comfortably furnished with everything I needed. The sand driveway led to a carport attached to the side of the mobile home, offering a bit of shade from the hot Southwest Florida sun. A sprawling Live Oak tree gave additional relief from the heat, and a grove of Sabal palms stood guard over the lanai. Occasionally, a flock of green parrots would settle into the trees, their raucous calls announcing their arrival. A front-row view of Lemon Bay was the icing on the cake. It was a slice of heaven. It was also the place where heaven came down and profoundly changed my life.

For weeks, the Father had been cutting deeper and deeper into my heart. I sat on the couch in the mornings and spent time reading the Bible and talking with him. During these sessions, he removed layer after layer off of my heart as if peeling an onion.

I remember the Father saying to me, "Tim, I want you to

trust me for this area of your life." I replied, "Father, I hear what you are saying. I know you want me to trust you, but, honestly, right now, I can't do that." I figured he would understand. But no. Instead of letting me off the hook, he pressed his thumb on me even harder. For a few days, I was miserable. The pressure smothered me. Would I trust him or not? Finally, after several days spent wrestling in misery, I relented. "Okay, Father," I said, "I will trust you for this."

Where I felt despair, now I felt joy. I was trusting God! A renewed excitement for life filled me. I was stunned to see myself trusting him in that area. I celebrated this newly found trust in God as I went about my day.

Then, days later, I was sitting on the couch, reading the Bible and praying, when the Father said to me, "Okay, Tim, now I need you to trust me for this area of your life." Again I replied, "Father, I believe you are asking me to trust you, but I'm just going to be completely honest and tell you I can't trust you in that area right now." And so, the cycle continued. For a few days, I was depressed. I finally broke and submitted to him. I surrendered to him. I found his strength to trust him in that area. Joy replaced despair. I was elated for a few days, celebrating this new level of trust, until once again, he asked me to trust him more fully. Again the rollercoaster plummeted to the bottom.

This cycle went on for over thirty days. It was an out-of-control ride of emotional highs and lows. It exhausted me. I was concerned I was having a mental health issue. So I scheduled an appointment with a Christian counselor who was a friend of mine. I shared with him the emotional highs and lows I had been riding. He listened intently. Finally, I closed my plea saying, "I just want to know if I need medication."

He sat there for a moment, lips pursed, eyes glancing off to the side, as the phrase hung in the air. Then, after a long pause, he looked at me and spoke. "Tim," he said, "there is a difference between being depressed and being broken. And I'm telling you I'm sitting across from someone whom God is trying to break."

His words resonated with me. I felt the Holy Spirit speaking through him. I decided at that moment the next time God took me down, I was not getting up until he finished the work in me.

That time came a few days later. Once again, I sensed the Father was asking me to trust him fully. When you have experienced childhood trauma, trust does not come easily. While I knew God understood this, it was clear the time had come to let go and trust him completely.

I want to say it was an easy conversation. It was not. I lay on the floor of that tiny trailer with my face on the carpet, hands extended over my head, and wept. The box in my heart where I kept my insecurities shattered. Fear spilled out onto the floor. Shame oozed out like puss pressed from a wound. It was ugly and beautiful at the same time. For in that moment of brokenness, pure love was poured into my life, flushing out all the impurities. All the lies, all the shame, all the self-doubt and disgust, all came flooding out as my body trembled. I don't know how long I lay there. I do remember coming to a place of stillness. I was lying on the floor. I turned my head to the side and rested my head on the carpet. My breathing slowed. A hush settled in the room. And then it happened.

I struggle to communicate what I experienced because I am not completely clear on what happened. All I know is that humble little trailer filled with the love of the Father. I have not experienced anything like it before or since. It was the purest love I have ever known. It washed over me like a tsunami. It flooded every crack and crevice in the room. The air was heavy and thick with it as if I could reach out my hand and draw my fingers through it. I didn't want to move. I could hardly breathe. It was pure love. It was as if the presence of God was filling the Temple. The Father himself had come into my tiny one-bedroom trailer as if it were the temple of the Most High God.

At that moment, I was a baby being bathed in the kitchen sink by his father. The father cradles the baby in the sink, supporting him with one hand, cupping warm water in the other, pouring over the child's head, gently washing away the impurities. The baby coos, smiling, eyes dancing, arms flailing, tiny fingers opening and closing in delight.

I lay there in perfect peace, all tension gone, my eyes rimmed with tears, this time from inexpressible love washing over me.

I remember not wanting to go to bed, assuming the feeling would disappear in the sunrise. But, eventually, I succumbed to sleep. I slept deeply, fully, and woke the next morning with a new sense of peace in my life.

Heaven had come down. I had experienced the love of the Father. And nothing would ever be the same.

The Great Mystery

A glaring question resurfaces when I consider traumatic events from my childhood. Where was the Father God when I was experiencing trauma as a child? I mean, if he loved me, wouldn't he have interceded? If he can fill me to the full with his love, why would he allow me to be hurt? Wouldn't he use every resource available to protect me? Why did he not do that?

It is one of the great mysteries of the universe. In my limited mental capacity, I am not confident I can adequately answer the question of where was God. But let me attempt in my simple way to explain my suspicion.

Where was the Father when I was experiencing trauma as a child? I believe he was there in the room with me. He saw everything that was happening. I imagine he watched with one hand clasped over his mouth, tears streaming down his face, witnessing firsthand the effect of sin in the world. His precious creation, twisted, damaged, destroyed, and all because of sin. All because of a wretched enemy who only longs to destroy and to kill.

The Father also knew he had already made a way for me to reconnect with him as a father and child. As he watched with horror the effect of sin at that moment, he understood one day I would discover him as Father. And when I experienced his love to the full, everything would change.

He understood that the depth of the Universal Ache in my life would be the depth of love he would fill me with. The breadth of the Father-shaped hole would be the breadth of the love that would fill the cavern. The deeper the hole, the deeper the filling. It is possible that the depth of the Father's love in my life today is directly relative to the depth of pain I endured as a child. My wounded state, a benefit.

Furthermore, the love I have for the Father is born out of an understanding of *my* sin and the effect it had on my life. The choices I made while trying to overcome the effects of my childhood trauma are mine alone. The patterns of sin I chose, in my vain attempt to fill the void, were my own undoing. I can't blame anyone for my choices. My sin was just as bad, for it separated me from the Father. My choices led me farther and farther from him, farther from healing, farther from his love. It was when I understood the depth of my own sin that I was overwhelmed with love for the Father. The Bible says "he who is forgiven little, loves little." When I have a problem loving the Father, it is likely I have difficulty understanding the depth of my depravity.

In the end, the love of the Father began to heal my wounds. Day after day, hour after hour, I sat upon his lap, held tightly in his loving embrace. Most of the time, I sat in silence. I sat in stillness. No words needed. No conversation necessary. Only love. Pure love washing over me, again and again. Filling me, overwhelming me. Little by little, old wounds healing. In time, even the scars fading away. Whole. Filled to the full with his love.

We are told that if we're beautiful, if we're skinny, if we're successful, famous, if we fit in, if everyone loves us we'll be happy. But that's not entirely true.

—Cara Delevingne
Fashion model and actress

Chapter 11

The Father Who Heals Our Shame

For many years, I felt like I was living two lives. One was overtly public, the other extremely private. I kept them as far apart as possible. Publicly, I traveled extensively, speaking in churches and conferences around the United States and Canada. On occasion, I ministered internationally, traveling to almost every continent. On average, I was home about ten days a month. My public life was on display, and it took a lot of effort to keep up the façade.

My public persona is Timothy Mark, author, speaker, adventurer, gregarious, smiling, warm, inviting. He is outgoing, lover of the Father, lover of people, striving after holiness and relationship with the Father. He plants prayer gatherings, helping others to learn how to hear the voice of the Father. This is the persona most people know.

Meanwhile, my private persona is simply Tim. This Tim is a recluse, rarely leaving the house, comfortable being alone. He used to download porn on occasion. He loves raunchy insult comedy but rarely indulges because he believes it harms his relationship with the Father. In a gathering, he prefers the corner of a room rather than the center of the action. Being around people quickly tires him. He recharges when he is alone. He is content to spend time in solitude, working in his garden. He highly values deep personal relationships with a few core friends.

For many years, one single thought kept my two personas apart: shame. I was keenly aware of my failures. Past sin haunted me. I thought if people knew Tim – the Tim who was a sex addict, the Tim who was a failure in relationships – they would be shocked. I felt I had to keep up appearances. It kept me from growing as a child of the Father. But once I understood the universal nature of my thoughts and behaviors, it set me free to share openly. Shame melted away. I found it exhilarating to know my failures could encourage others. I understood the Father could use even my failures for good in helping other brothers and sisters to find the Father's healing love as well.

The key was becoming comfortable with Tim, the one I tend to hide from others. Not comfortable with sin, but rather with my humanity. That is where I am now, resting in peace on the lap of God. On his lap, I found a father who knew the private Tim and loved him anyway.

Shame is a powerful force. It arises from a sense of dishonor over something we have done. Shame deadbolts us into an underground chamber, hidden in darkness. Shame creates a prison out of the fear of being exposed for who we are, and we lock ourselves inside. We craft a carefully curated exterior in the hope no one will discover our true identity or what we believe our identity to be. Shame whispers to us, "You are unworthy to experience love." It tattoos itself unto our identity, and we falsely believe no one would love us if they knew our secrets. But this is a lie. It is simply not true.

Coming Home

Shame also keeps us from receiving the love of the Father. But it is not the Father who is preventing us from receiving his love. Our shame prevents it. Jesus even spoke of this in a story he told.

In the story, there was a wealthy Jewish farmer who had two sons. One day, the younger son asked his father to give him his future inheritance now. Remarkably, the father agreed and split the estate between the two sons.

The younger son was ecstatic. He took his share and left, traveling far from home. The farther, the better, he thought. Then he would be free to spend the money on whatever his heart desired. No one at home would be the wiser. Free of his restrictive family, he held nothing back. Women, alcohol, pleasure, you name it. If it lit his fire, he indulged. For a long time, he was on a high. But the day came when all the money was gone.

Now the son was in trouble. With no money, he needed a job. But there was a famine and little work available. The only job he could find was working for a hog farmer. His job was to feed the pigs out in the field. Now, remember, according to Jewish law, pigs are unclean. Just touching one makes a person unclean. But it was the only job he could find. So he went from living the high life to this. And he was starving. Even the corn cobs he was feeding to the pigs looked appetizing. But no one gave him anything.

Finally, emaciated, his frame hollowed by hunger, he had enough. He had squandered his father's estate. He had violated his family code of conduct. Filthy pigs were eating better than he was. With no choice left, he turned to home.

It is hard to comprehend how difficult this decision must have been. Imagine the shame he now felt. He had spent his entire inheritance down to zero. He was tending pigs. He had nothing left but shame. Shame sat proudly at the top of the mess. It clung to him like a backpack, smirking at him as he plodded home. What would his father think?

As he walked, he rehearsed in his mind what he would say upon his return. "Father, I have sinned against heaven and before you. I am no longer worthy to be called your son. Treat me as one of your hired servants."

Then a startling thing happened. While the young man was still a long way off from his father's home, his father saw him. At first, the father could not believe what he was seeing. It was difficult to make out for sure, but he thought he recognized his son's gait. Surely it was not true. He had looked to the horizon from the day his precious son had left, longing for his return. Could it be his son was coming home? The father started walking toward the image, squinting in the harsh afternoon sun. Then, as his boy came into clear focus, he began to run. He ran with all his might. His heart exploded in his chest, not from exertion but from love. His son had returned! When at last they collided on the open field, the father threw his arms around his son and clung to him. He wept, running his fingers through his son's hair, kissing his face. His son had returned!

At first, the son did not know how to respond. He could not look his father in the eyes. He looked down, avoiding his father's gaze. He stiffened, not sure if he should return the embrace. In his mind, he was no longer a son. Finally, he blurted out the statement he had rehearsed over the endless hours of treading home. "Father," he said, "I've blown it. I made a huge mess of things. I'm not even worthy of being called your son. I only want a job with the other hired servants. That is all I am asking."

But the father would have none of it. He drew back, holding the face of his son in his hands, and without moving his gaze, he shouted to his servant, "Quickly, bring the best clothes and get these rags off of him. Put a ring on his hand, and get some shoes for his feet. And tell the staff to prepare a feast. We are celebrating tonight! My son, who was dead, is alive! He was lost, but now he is found." And they began to celebrate.

There is more to the story. But for this moment, pause and consider the difference in perspective between our two characters. The wayward child allows shame to rename him. He gives up his identity as a son and exchanges it for that of a hired worker. Shame steals his identity. The father, for his part, will have none of it. He had looked to the horizon since the moment he watched his son walk away. He had waited for what felt like an eternity to embrace him. The boy never ceased being his son, and the father never stopped loving him. Wasting the money didn't change that fact. Wasting his life didn't change that truth. The only thing that mattered was his son was finally back, safe in his embrace.

Understand that from the moment we walk away from the Father God, he never stops longing for us to return. Never. He looks to the horizon, aching to dwell with us. He longs to have us back with him, back in his embrace, back upon his lap, sharing time with him. For our part, we fall for the lie from shame. We give up our identity as sons and daughters and exchange it for the identity of a servant. We come back to the Father God but in a sort of subservient way. "Father," we say, "I am no longer worthy of being called your son. I am content only to be your servant." But the Father God will have none of it. No! He never gives up the identity he created for us. We are his sons! We are his daughters! We are his children! And his love for us never ends.

When we feel shame, we hide. It is natural. It is part of our DNA. Adam and Eve hid when they sinned. Like Adam and Eve, our natural reaction is to cover up so we will not be exposed.

We hide from everyone our most profound failings, our crippling fears, and our abject inability to live holy, perfect lives. We hide from one another. We hide from the Father.

Sadly, no one benefits from this behavior. We do not benefit personally. We create our own solitary prisons. And others do not benefit from finding a community of people like them who also have failed. We help no one. The enemy is the only one who succeeds.

Shame burrows into our spirit like a tick, leaving behind a toxic infection that is difficult to remove. It is like Lyme disease. The infection begins with the smallest of moments, a moment of failure, a moment of loss, even a moment of abuse. Then, it buries itself deep within every cell of our bodies. We try to purge it. We think we are making progress. Then it flares up again, setting us back.

For most of my life, I have lived with shame hiding in the background. I covered it up with a smile and a laugh, but for as long as I can remember, it has lurked in the dark corners of my mind, waiting to present itself at the opportune time.

In the early years of my career, I was a singer/songwriter. Of all the songs I have composed, one is my particular favorite. It is not a pop-hit. But it tells my story, my struggle with shame. I titled it "Stumble."

Stumble

On a journey marked with failure
When I count regrets I've had my share
And of the roads that I have taken
With shame as my companion, I'm aware
But I have found a path that leads me to forgiveness
Upon my knees, at my Father's feet

Chorus
For I am only human,
not some hero of the faith
I'm merely an example
of God's mercy and his grace
I keep my eyes on Jesus
when my gains become a loss
As I stumble to the cross

So let us keep our eyes on Jesus
The author and perfector of our faith
Who for the joy set before him
Endured the cross, despising its shame
For he is seated at the right hand of the Father
To intercede for you and me

Chorus
For I am only human,
not some hero of the faith
I'm merely an example
of God's mercy and his grace
I keep my eyes on Jesus
when my gains become a loss
As I stumble to the cross

So let us keep our eyes on Jesus

Jesus bore our shame on himself when he paid the penalty for all our sins on the cross. He died to remove the sting of shame from within us. His death and resurrection set us free from shame.

This thought helped me so much. Finally, the cure for my

shame spread through every cell of my body, rooting out the guilt, cleansing every memory, washing me clean.

When I discovered the safe place of being on the lap of the Father, my shame melted away. No longer did I feel I needed to hide. Instead, my failures became trophies of his grace and mercy. I could accept my failures because the Father accepted me. His embrace was all that mattered; his healing touch, my singular longing.

I found myself on the lap of God, leaning back into his embrace. I was weary from years of trying to maintain appearances. I sat there, breathing in, breathing out, letting him hold me, quietly resting. With halting words, I shared my failures with him, one after another, ugly, horrid deeds, incomprehensible acts of sin.

He let me speak, not saying a word. But as I spoke, his arms tightened around me. I felt something on the crown of my head, something wet, and realized he was crying. I choked on my words, and my sentence trailed off into silence. All shame was gone, melted away. In its place, pure love poured into my heart in a torrent.

I had found the Father who heals our shame.

Be still, and know that I am God.

—*The Father God*

Chapter 12

Learning to Be Still

My elementary art teacher was the first to inspire me in the creative arts. She worked with me outside of class, molding my skills, critiquing my drawings. She made me believe I could be an artist as a career. I developed my talent through middle and high school, looking towards college with an eye on a degree in Fine Art. I was hoping to land a job as a designer. When I mentioned my interest to folks in our church community, the response surprised me. "Are you going to be a chalk artist?" they would ask. A chalk artist was someone who did presentations in churches using chalk art to illustrate biblical truth. This career path was the furthest thing from my mind. I stood blinking at the individual, unsure how to respond to this career suggestion.

My church culture expected me to use my abilities and talents for the church. It was frowned upon to pursue a career outside of that sphere. If you got a degree in education, church members expected you to teach in a Christian school. Everything turned back to some sort of ministry focus. To be an artist and make great art for the sake of making great art would be wasting God-given talent.

To serve God was to be loved by him. Service was the key to receiving his love. So we worked, we served, sacrificing family and weekends, always striving to serve him better, never quite achieving success. The Father's perfect love was always just slightly out of reach.

I thought I had to be busy serving God to be loved by him. Serving God was all that mattered. In the conservative church in which I grew up, those who committed their lives to missionary work were highly esteemed. The successful entrepreneur was also held in high esteem, but only because of his or her ability to provide the cash needed to send the missionary. Being the missionary was the ticket. If I wanted to be loved by God, I needed to do something to earn his love.

Our culture has embedded the idea we need to do something to have value. What we do gives us worth. We have been programmed from childhood to think being busy is the highest goal. "How have you been?" we ask. "I've been busy," is the standard reply. The answer shares no details, no depth of relationship. Being busy is the stain of the North American mindset. We must be active. To sit still would appear to be lazy. As a result, Americans work more hours per week than people in any other country.

Because I work from home, I have this underlying perception that my neighbors think I am lazy. They don't see me leaving for a job, so they must think I am retired. At least, that is my perception. When I see them, I find myself sharing a list of the things I am working on. But I am not updating them on my life. Instead, I am trying to convince them I am busy. Busy. The North American standard of a contributing member of society.

In my warped perception of life, I labored for acceptance, to feel loved. I wrapped the idea in a robe of perfection, always striving, never able to rest, waiting for the other shoe to fall, trying to prevent the chaos, if possible, constantly living in a state of high alert. And what has all this busyness brought me? Stress, feeling like I can never quite catch up. Lying awake at night unable to turn off my brain. Always longing for a place of rest somewhere over the rainbow, but never quite able to get there.

This unconscious striving manifested itself with high blood pressure, burnout, and many health issues just below the surface. I carried this idea into my relationship with the Father God as well. I must be busy serving him to please him.

My early conversations with the Father tended to follow this pattern. "What do you want me to do for you today?" was a common refrain. It was answered with silence, with a nudge and slightly tighter embrace, silently asking me to settle in and be still. I squirmed, wanting to get off his lap, to do something for him, wanting to please him, aching for his love. When I fidgeted, he held me closer. In the beginning, it felt stressful to just sit there on his lap. Instinctively, I needed to serve him. Serving was the key to love. Oh, how I longed for his love. Surely there was something I could do that would please him, to make him smile upon me.

But all the Father wanted was to spend time with me, to hold me, to love me as I am, his child. In time, I learned to be still, to accept a love freely given to me solely because I was his child. Little by little, I became comfortable just being with him, sitting quietly on his lap, leaning back into his embrace, smothered with his love. The more I sat with him, the more I released the stress of wanting to serve him. Little by little, my projects fell like toys to the floor.

Just being with him became the highest privilege. Closing my eyes, leaning back, feeling his embrace, experiencing a love I had never known. Where once I had strained to get on with the project I had designed to please him, I now rested comfortably in his embrace. If he needed something, he would let me know. For now, he just wanted to dwell with me, to be with me, to love me.

What Matters Most

During this season of my life, while writing this book, I have applied for work at the McMurdo research base in Antarctica. It is a grand dream to experience the remote, frozen continent. Over the past few months, I interviewed and received an alternate contract with the United States Antarctica Program. The alternate status means I am under contract, but I do not have a permanent position yet. I am an alternate. If a primary contract employee cannot go for any reason, I am next in line to fill the position. My contract is with the Lodging Department. I am available to fill any position within this department, but my status is an alternate for a steward position. A steward is a nice way of saying janitor.

This morning in my time with the Father, I spoke with him about my alternate status with the team preparing for Antarctica. The issue hounds me. I envy the folks who have primary status. I am connected with other employees online. When I scroll down the page of posts of team members with primary contracts, I am excited for them and frustrated at the same time. Management has set their plans in place. As an alternate, I prepare as if I am going, with no idea if it will happen. I have scrutinized the gear needed down to the specific fabric content of the recommended base layers. Curriers deliver packages from online orders to my front porch almost daily. A storage bin in the back of my closet, dedicated to McMurdo, is overflowing at this point. But the one thing I cannot purchase is peace over not yet having a job placement. Over the past few days, I have talked with the Father about my longing for a primary position. I have asked him to give me a job placement. I have told him how unsettled I feel in the process of waiting. I have asked for a resolution, not because I want a specific job, but because I want certainty.

But this morning, my mindset changed. As I sat meditating and praying, the Father reminded me of the joy of experiencing his presence sitting quietly on his lap. The manifest presence of the Father during the everyday moments of life is a treasure. To know he is near brings me joy. When his love washes over me, the things that are not vital fade away, and the critical things come clearly into focus. Distinguishing between the two is crucial to understanding the peace the Father longs for us to experience.

When the Father reminded me of his presence with me, suddenly the room felt illuminated, lighter, carefree, or at least care-less. At that moment, whether I even went to Antarctica did not matter. If I got a job assignment, or what placement I got did not matter. Only the presence of the Father mattered. Suddenly, praying for these things seemed frivolous. The Bible says, "My thoughts are not your thoughts, neither are your ways my ways, declares the Lord. For as the heavens are higher than the earth, so are my ways higher than your ways and my thoughts than your thoughts."

The Father thinks thoughts far different from mine. To flip the script, my thoughts are lower than the Father's thoughts. My ways are lower than his ways. I am a "low thinker." I am concerned about job placement. The Father is a "high thinker." The Father is concerned about drawing his kids closer to himself. He longs to dwell with them. Remember, the thought of dwelling with us consumes him. The key is to learn to think like he thinks, prioritizing thoughts of his presence with me. I focus on the one thing that matters: sitting still with him. When

I do this, I find the other things I thought were so important are not. Suddenly it no longer matters what job I get, or even if I go at all. All that matters is dwelling with the Father wherever he leads. Today, at this moment, I sit quietly on his lap. Tomorrow, whatever may come, I choose to dwell with him. I practice the priority of his presence and nothing else.

This is not to say my low thoughts do not matter to the Father. It is just that he sees them in the proper context. It is the difference between how a toddler thinks and how a father thinks. A toddler thinks about what will make him happy at the moment. If he wants a toy, he will cry if he doesn't get it. All that matters is his happiness at that specific moment.

The father understands, but he also is thinking about the health and safety of the child. The father is thinking higher thoughts. The child is thinking low thoughts. The father loves the child and loves doing things to make the child happy. But the father is always aware of the higher issues – the health and wellness of the child. The happiness of the child is far less a concern.

You Make Me Happy

There have been a handful of times when I heard the Father whispering to me, and the word impacted me so profoundly that I remember when and where I was when it happened. Such is the case for a moment in Asia I will never forget.

I had flown halfway around the world to Singapore on a spur-of-the-moment decision. A few weeks earlier, I had met a man from the island nation while I was speaking at a family conference in New Hampshire. During breaks, we had long conversations about what God was doing in his home country. Some of the stories he shared were remarkably similar to how I was seeing God at work in the prayer gatherings here. He invited me to come and see what God was doing with their gatherings. Something in my spirit said I should go. And so, a few weeks later, my flight landed in the garden city of Singapore.

Meeting with the believers there was humbling. When they gathered to pray, they cried out to the Father with abandon. We set aside differences in theology, preferring to love our Father with abandon and to love one another regardless of the differences. I treasure the memories of those gatherings.

One gathering, in particular, stands out to me. The room was small, only large enough to accommodate about thirty people. The leader had set up a few chairs in a semi-circle. I sat in the second row of seats, preferring the background, not wanting to insert myself into their gathering. I listened as one after another they cried out to the Father. The presence of God filled the room. My heart joined with them, relishing the love of God. In that quiet moment, the Father spoke to me so clearly, so distinctly, that it astounded me.

"Tim," he said, "you make me happy."

It was all he said. But it was one of the most meaningful words I have ever heard him say to me. The thought that I made the Father happy stunned me. Tears welled up in my eyes. It was more than I could ask to imagine that somehow, in my simple little toddler-like relationship with him, I made him happy.

Within the heart of every child is a profound desire to know their father is proud of them. In my broken state, I did not recall hearing those words before. I always felt like I could never quite measure up. I only remembered comments that belittled me, that cut me down. To have the Father God say to me, "You make me happy," left me speechless. I sat there, eyes widening, heart racing, shocked into silence by the phrase. I clung to the words. I held them close to my heart, feeling their warmth spreading through my veins. The prayer gathering continued, but I heard little of it. I only heard the voice of the Father, speaking so lovingly to me.

The Father said something similar to his son Jesus on two separate occasions. Early in his public life, Jesus was baptized. The Bible says, at the time, a voice from heaven said, "You are my dearly loved Son, and you bring me great joy." Some gathered nearby thought they heard thunder. There it was, the voice of the Father God, thundering from the heavens, declaring, "My Son, I love you. You make me happy."

It happened a second time when Jesus was on the mountain with Peter, James, and John. The Bible says, "even as [Jesus] spoke, a bright cloud overshadowed them, and a voice from the cloud said, 'This is my dearly loved Son, who brings me great joy. Listen to him.'"

God built into our DNA the desire to know our parents are proud of us. As children, we approach our parents with our crayon drawings. We extend them out to them, longing for their approval. When they place our pictures on the fridge, the gallery of all good children's art, they communicate their pride in us. We beam with joy to see our efforts rewarded in this way.

What Makes the Father Happy?

And so, I wondered, what was it that made the Father happy? In that moment of the prayer gathering, why would he say to me, "You make me happy." I wasn't serving him. I wasn't even participating in the prayer gathering except in silent, personal prayer. I wasn't in Singapore to speak at a conference. I had no ministry opportunities there. So what had made him smile?

What is it that makes the Father beam with pride when he thinks of us? Again, I turned to the Bible to see what I could find. I found a father who just wants us to love him fully, with abandon, as if nothing else matters. I observed it in the Old

Testament, and I saw it repeated in the New Testament. There is one command higher than all others: Love the Lord your God with all your heart, all your soul, all your mind, and all your strength. "Just love me!" he cries.

So if I focused my life on just sitting on his lap, loving him with all my heart, all my soul, all my mind, would that be enough? What if everything else – serving him, living a pure life, loving others – all flowed out of this one thing?

For most of my life, I thought I had to serve God to make him happy. I thought if I were in ministry, somehow I would merit his love. What I did for him was of the highest importance. We commonly pray, "God, show me what you want me to do for you. What is your will for my life?" The Father hears our prayers, but then he reminds us we make him happy when we dwell with him like he intended, when we love him with all our heart, all our mind, all our strength. Our hearts, madly in love with him and fully surrendered; this is what makes him happy.

It was the great undoing in my life to let go of the idea that serving God was what made him happy. It was when I discovered the secret treasure of sitting in stillness on his lap, loving him with abandon, that I began to understand what the Father God intended all along.

This is not to say that serving God does not matter. But our service naturally follows our love. The order is what is important. We make the focus of our lives to love the Father with abandon, to surrender fully to his embrace, to spend time upon his lap in a relationship with him. This is what makes him proud of us. Then, and only then, should we even consider the idea of serving him. Our love for him must be preeminent. Our service for him is always secondary. Always.

Remember the story of the Jewish father and the two sons from the previous chapter? The second son had a lesson to learn as well.

Word of the wayward son's return spread quickly through the household and a celebration broke out. Now the older son was out working in one of the fields. As he was heading in, he heard the music and dancing.

"What on earth is going on?" he asked one of the servants.

"Your brother has come home," the servant replied, "and your dad is throwing a party."

The older son's jaw fell open in shock. Anger surged through him, veins bulging in his neck. He could not believe what was happening. "Are you kidding me?" he thought. He threw down his shovel in disgust and stood there, refusing to go in. Finally, one of the servants told the father what was happening. The father quietly slipped away from the party and headed out to the field to see his son. Oh, how he loved him. He wanted him to join the festivities, but the older son would have none of it. "Look," the son yelled, "I have worked for you all these years, and I have always done everything you told me to do. Yet you never threw a party for me! But, no, this so-called son of yours spends all your money on whores, and you throw a party for him."

The father looked longingly at the older son. His heart ached for him. Finally, he spoke. "Son, you are always with me, and all that is mine is yours. It was appropriate to celebrate today, for your brother was dead and is now alive. He was lost and is now found." With this, he turned and slowly walked back to the house.

What fascinates me in this story is the love of the father. He loved both of his sons equally. In both cases, he pursues his sons. He longs for each one to experience his love. The father is aware the older son is also struggling with his identity. After listening to the older son's tirade, the first thing the father says in reply is, "Son." He reminds him of his identity as a son. He is a son, not a servant.

Remember, our identity matters. Each had lost their identity as sons. The first son was willing to abandon his identity as a son because of shame. But the older son, who stayed home, also gave up his identity as a son. He lost his identity because of service. When he speaks to the father, he reminds him of his service and obedience, not his love. He has confused serving the father with loving the father. As a result, he also lost his identity as a son. It was taken not by shame but by servitude.

If we are not careful, we also trade our identity as sons and daughters for that of servants. Some confuse serving God with having a relationship with the Father God, but they are two completely different things. The irony is, it is entirely possible to serve God and not have a relationship with him. Jesus said many people think they will be with him in heaven because they serve him, but they will be shocked to hear him say, "Depart from me, I never knew you." They served God but had no personal relationship with him. This thought should terrify us.

Understand, it is possible to serve the Father without a relationship with him. However, it is impossible to have a deep, loving relationship with the Father God and not desire to serve him. Our service to him follows our love for him. When we experience his love, we naturally want others to experience it as well. We tell others how he transforms our lives through his love. Serving him becomes a natural expression of the relationship.

Remember, the entirety of the Bible is bookended with a father who wants to dwell with his kids. This is what makes him happy. For me to settle in upon his lap, to dwell with him, to surrender to his embrace, this is what matters. I give up trying to serve him to earn his love and simply love him with all my heart.

I come to the Father wondering how I can make him proud. I let go of my toys and crawl onto his lap. He lifts me unto his knee and brushes a hair from my face. I reach up with my tiny hand to feel the stubble on his chin. He laughs. He smiles as he looks into my eyes. I collapse onto his chest, feeling the warmth of his breath on the back of my neck. All is lost in the moment. All concern is stripped away as his chest rises and falls beneath me. I am a child with his father. He holds me. I rest in stillness on his lap. At this moment, nothing else matters. His thoughts become my thoughts. And the things I thought were important suddenly seem so far away, so distant, in a muffled haze.

In the stillness of the moment, I realize I have forgotten what I wanted to ask.

*No temptation has overtaken you
that is not common to man.*

*—Paul
First-century leader of the Church*

Chapter 13

Embracing Our Weaknesses

I have shared openly in these pages, not to be titillating, but to show you are not alone in your struggles. Perhaps, like me, you have struggled with an addiction like pornography. You may feel trapped in an unhealthy relationship pattern. The shame of this has kept you in silence. Reading my journey, you realize you are not alone. You can share your story with a trusted friend. You can find healing. But I am not writing this for the one who shares my background with porn or any other addictive behavior. Ultimately, the issue is not porn or our addiction. The problem is the Father-shaped hole. I write for all of us trying to fill the Father-shaped void, the Universal Ache. We are together on this journey.

Our enemy tempts us to fill the emptiness with food, drugs, alcohol, or social media. He draws us to fill the space with relationships, success, or significance. Any number of issues apply. The point is it is common. We are not as unique as we think we are. You are not alone in your struggle. We are in this together.

Through the years, I have sat with friends and listened to their stories. Stories of being molested as a child. Reports of abuse at the hands of a loved one. Shocking tales of incest. Pastors meet me in the parking lot after an event, looking around to see if anyone from their congregation is watching, and then share their addiction to pornography. Secrets held close, heavily guarded by shame. Often, our self-talk sounds like this: What would people think if they knew? I couldn't possibly share my struggle with anyone. I might lose my job.

Name your temptation. It is common. Let that sink in. You are not alone. You are in the majority. Understanding this truth takes power from our temptations. We are not struggling alone. We are working with many, many others with the exact same temptation. My temptation may be different from yours, but that does not mean I am alone. It just means I am not sharing with someone who is in my camp. My temptation is not unique to me. I am not the only one dealing with it. Add to this the notion that most people will not honestly share their weakness, and suddenly you think you are the only one the enemy has tempted in this area. It is a lie. Your temptation is quite common. It's just that no one wants to talk about it.

Further, there is a difference between being tempted to sin and sinning. Often, we treat the temptation as a blow to our confidence. But we should remember temptation is common to the human condition. Whatever your temptation is, it is not unusual. It is common. The enemy would have you believe otherwise, but he is a liar, the father of lies.

Sharing Our Struggles

This feeling that I was alone in my struggle kept me in bondage to porn for many years. I was never a daily user. I was more like a binge drinker. I would not look at any porn for months. But the hunger for more images would linger in the pit of my stomach. Usually, I resisted. I would pray for God to help me to live a holy and pure life. Then, tired from ministry work, emotionally drained from a long trip away from home, I would sit down at my computer with no one around. I made sure the window blinds were closed. I didn't want my neighbor to see what I was getting into. Usually, I began with images that were on the edge of inappropriate. Technically not porn, but definitely softly blowing on the embers in my gut. One click deeper into the abyss. Then another. Then a cascade of horrid images. Dopamine flooded my veins. The rush of adrenaline felt wonderful.

As with any addiction, I exchanged lesser drugs for the cocaine of extreme porn. After a time, the dopamine effect wears off with the same images, so I searched out the extremes to get another hit. Users of porn will understand what I am talking about. Because the images get more and more extreme, the shame factor only deepens. Usually, this would continue for a few hours. Then, the drug no longer satisfying, I would stop. Shame cascaded over me like a waterfall. I had blown it again. Again! Would I ever be free from this cycle? I cleared my browser cache. I cleared my search history. I prayed for forgiveness. And I prayed for healing that never seemed to come.

Finally, I could take it no more. Tentatively, I share my mess with my brother. To say those words out loud was incredibly difficult. The shame was so immense. What would he think? What would anyone think? My pulse raced. I stammered around the topic for a moment, circling in, testing the waters to see how he would react. Then, finally, I shared the depth of my shame.

I expected to feel even more shame having spoken the words out loud. Instead, what I found was freedom. Yes, freedom. It felt like the bondage of the addiction was broken in half. Just saying the words out loud lifted the weight I had been carrying alone. Someone I respected and loved understood. My secret was out! I no longer had to hide.

I shared my addiction with other trusted friends and a remarkable thing happened. Each time I shared my story, it broke the bondage in half again. I began alone, carrying the weight of my sin by myself. When I shared with my brother, I split the load with him. Then I shared my story with a friend and I felt even more relief from the bondage. I shared it with another friend. Again, I experienced even more relief from the bondage. Over and over, I shared. I found a brotherhood of others who were also in the fight. Finally, I shared my story at men's conferences, now completely open and public with my shame.

What I found was healing. I was fleshing out the Bible where it says, "Share your faults one with another, and you will be healed."

Sharing my story with others was an essential part of the process. Sharing my story with the Father completed the deal.

It is important to understand that while the bondage was gone, the temptation was still there. I am still a guy. I have a normal level of testosterone flowing through my veins. Even though the bondage was gone, often I experienced a pang of hunger to return to my old ways. It was like something stirred deep in my gut. It bothered me a lot. I understood that my temptation was common among men. But I felt there was still something deep inside me where I needed healing. Something felt like it needed to be fixed. Something hidden deep within me still percolated.

I was sitting below deck on my sailboat when I had a conversation with the Father about this feeling that something was still broken. The sun had long since set, and the light of the moon was filtering into the cabin through the portlights. There was no one around. An evening breeze stirred in the companionway. I sat in the silence and spoke to the Father.

"You know, Father," I said, "I don't understand why I still feel like there is a hunger deep within me to binge on porn. I've seen such progress in this area, and I feel like you have set me free. But at the same time, I feel like something is broken deep inside of me. I don't know what it is. I don't have to know what's wrong with me. I just want you to fix it. Go into the deepest part of my heart and heal what needs to be healed. Change what needs to be changed. I do not have to be part of the process. I don't need to understand what you are doing. Please, just do it. Go into the deepest part of my life and change me."

The prayer could not have lasted longer than sixty seconds. There was no crying, no wailing, or gnashing of teeth. But there was surrender.

At that moment, I gave up trying to fix myself and fully yielded to my loving Father. I gave him permission to go into the deepest part of me, without explanation, and have all of me. To this day, I cannot explain what happened. I do not know what he did. He has never explained it to me. But at that moment, something changed. From that point forward, the hunger left. There is no longer an ache to search the internet for images. I cannot find words to explain how profoundly my life changed.

Again, yes, I still have testosterone flowing through my veins. I have a normal sex drive. But the addictive nature is gone. Completely. The Father God healed me in a moment. Prior to this point, my prayer had been for God to help me live a holy and pure life. But that is praying for God to work on the edges. That is praying for the Father to heal the symptoms. First, I needed healing of the cause of my unholiness and impurity. And when that was complete, then holiness and purity followed.

This is why sitting on the lap of God matters! We come to

him with our mess. We sit with him and share our deepest secrets. Instead of working on the symptoms, he touches on the need. He heals the cause of our addictions. When that is complete, then we are free to live the life we always longed for – sitting on the lap of God.

When I sit on the lap of God, he wraps his arms around me. I lean back into his chest. I am safe in his embrace. "What's on your mind," he says. I hesitate to share. It is a mess. What will he think? Saying the words out loud frightens me. Finally, I speak.

"Father, I've blown it. I am so discouraged. I look back at my life, and I am horrified by what I see. If anyone knew all the times I've looked at porn, they would be shocked. I am so ashamed. I don't know what to do."

There is a pause, and finally, he speaks. "I know," he says, "I've seen everything you've looked at." Another pause, but now I feel his embrace drawing me even closer. "What you are dealing with is quite common. You don't know this because no one wants to talk about things of which they are ashamed. I appreciate your honesty with me. Know that my grace is sufficient for you. I love you so much. I already forgave your sin. Now I need you to trust me to heal you in those areas."

At this moment, it is helpful to remember he already knows all our faults. He understands the shame we carry, and he knows the lies with which the enemy has defeated us.

Oddly, some of my favorite conversations with the Father revolve around my sin and shame. In the safety of his embrace, I can be honest. I pour out the darkest secrets of my heart to him. His response comforts me. "I know, Tim. I understand. I am aware of all you have done. I know the shame you carry. But you should know how much I love you. I already forgave you. You are my son. And I love you."

The Bible says Jesus, the Son of God, was in every respect

"tempted as we are, yet without sin. Let us then with confidence draw near to the throne of grace, that we may receive mercy and find grace to help in time of need." Because our enemy tempted the Son of God in every way possible, Jesus can relate to the temptations we face. He understands how common they are. And now, he is the one who intercedes to the Father on our behalf. Because of this, we can come to the Father, the one who sits on the throne of grace, and receive mercy and find grace to help in our time of need.

Our enemy wants us to believe we are alone in our battle with temptation. "What would people think," the devil whispers. "You couldn't possibly share your real self. You are alone." Remember, our enemy hates the Father. He will do anything he can to prevent the Father from having a relationship with us. So he tries to keep us isolated from others, alone in our fight for freedom, beaten down, separated from the Father. He wants to see our lives destroyed by the effects of sin. Nothing would make him happier. So he lies to us, telling us we are the only one who has struggled with a particular sin. Alone in our struggle, we never find healing. And we believe the lie that says we can never change.

Confession within Community

James, the brother of Jesus and an early Church leader wrote, "Confess your sins to one another and pray for one another, that you may be healed." In this simple phrase, we find the answer to the lie of isolation. We find healing in community. We find healing as we share our faults, our failures, the nagging temptations that assault us. We discover a community of others who long for healing, who fail, who pick themselves back up, and who crawl back unto the lap of the Father for more time with him, more time washed by his love, more healing of scars, more freedom from sin. We discover we are not alone. Our temptations are, in fact, common. We heal together, one with another. We confess to one another. We pray for one another.

Because our enemy also knows the Bible, he knows we will find healing when we confess our sins to one another. So he works overtime to prevent us from sharing. This is why he tries to isolate us. He whispers in our ear, "What would people think?" Your stomach tightens. Fear grows within.

Even as I write this, I imagine the fear you may experience just thinking of sharing your failures with someone. I understand. The thought terrified me as well. It kept me isolated from intimacy with others and intimacy with the Father. I shut down. I kept it to myself. Because I was ashamed of what I had done, I assumed others would shame me as well. But it was a lie. Instead, I found grace, comfort, brotherhood. I was frightened to share with my brother the struggle I was having with porn. But when finally I shared, a feeling of freedom washed over me. That feeling is what I want you to experience. The bondage cut in half. The weight lifted. A feeling of being able to breathe freely.

And so, we learn to share our faults with one another. We learn to share our shortcomings with the Father, the Father who understands our weaknesses. He knows how he made us. He remembers that we are dust. And so we crawl upon his lap. We share our failings with him. We find healing as we sit with him, his arms around us, his voice reassuring, his forgiveness healing us in places we cannot touch.

It's always sold as if everybody else's life is perfect. That's the problem. And therefore you think that if everyone else's life is perfect, there must be something wrong with me.

—*Prince Harry*
Duke of Suffex

Chapter 14

The View from His Lap

Weeks slowly passed as I waited to hear a word from my supervisor in Antarctica if a position opened up. Finally, it happened! I received a primary contract to serve the McMurdo community as a steward for the upcoming season. I was over the moon with excitement! This long-held dream was finally coming together. But as excitement raged, a nagging ache settled into my gut. A tension slipped in, a feeling that something was not quite right. The clock was ticking, and the day of departure for Antarctica was only a few weeks away.

I reviewed my journal of this journey over the past few months, noticing a disturbing trend. Again and again, I wrote about the anxiety I felt while getting the job and preparing to leave. A sense of tension seemed to be on repeat play. Throughout this season, there were many moments when I felt anxious. The dream was so big and challenging to attain. It is a rare handful of people who get the opportunity I have sought. Now, feeling so close to the finish line, I felt stressed instead of at peace.

For several years, I had felt overwhelmed by my multiple

responsibilities – the ministry, work outside of the ministry, owning a home, owning a vehicle, owning a sailboat – all of which needed attention and focus. Now, with deployment to Antarctica on the horizon, I felt like I was driving a car a hundred miles per hour, trying to bring it to a complete stop before I left. I was standing on the brake as hard as I could, but it felt like I was locked up and in a slide out of control. The perception filled me with anxiety over and over again.

I can give many logical reasons why I should not feel anxious. But anxiety doesn't respond to logic. Instead, anxiety glares at me, demanding my attention. When I lay down to sleep, it awakens, prodding me, imposing itself, stealing slumber and rest. Instead of shutting off, my brain turns on, trying to settle anxious thoughts that have rested in the background all day. The only way to break the cycle is to get up and read a book or watch TV until I finally feel able to go to sleep. This cycle happened to me in the process of getting the primary position at McMurdo. And I found it happening to me again as the days ticked down to deployment.

I had worked hard to check things off my list as I closed down my life for the time being. I had purchased all the items required, and my bags were still a few pounds under the allowed weight. But one essential thing remained unresolved – what to do with my sailboat.

In Florida, the winter months are the best months for sailing and living aboard the vessel. Most sailboat owners put their boats into safe storage during the summer hurricane season. It did not make sense to keep the sailboat since I would likely be working in Antarctica for the next few winters (i.e., the best time to live aboard and sail). So, I decided to sell it.

During this time, writing had been my primary focus. Now, with just weeks away from the expected departure, I was finally getting around to listing the boat for sale. Once again, a sense of

The View from His Lap

panic settled in. I began to feel anxious about it. Logically, I knew I could just put the boat in storage and manage it next year. But again, my anxiety does not respond to logic.

Anxiety gnawed at my gut. At the height of my concern, the Father reminded me of a verse I learned as a child. The Bible says, "do not be anxious about anything, but in everything by prayer and supplication with thanksgiving let your requests be made known to God. And the peace of God, which surpasses all understanding, will guard your hearts and your minds in Christ Jesus."

I looked up the verse and noticed an odd thing. In the English Standard Version, the phrase, "do not be anxious about anything..." begins in the lower case, implying it is in the middle of a thought or sentence. Curious, I looked up the whole passage to consider the context. There it was. The preceding phrase says, "The Lord is at hand." Read together it says this: "The Lord is at hand; do not be anxious about anything...."

I looked into the original language for the phrase "The Lord is at hand." Strong's Concordance defines the word *lord* this way: he to whom a person or thing belongs, about which he has the power of deciding; master, lord, or the possessor and disposer of a thing.

The discovery shocked me. The answer to my anxiety appeared in a straightforward phrase: "He to whom a person or thing belongs." Those words exposed the heart of my fear. The glaring truth is I was attempting to play God. But God alone is Lord. I belong to him.

Further, everything in my care belongs to him. I am merely the steward. I take care of his things the best I can. Even my body is his. I cannot change myself. I cannot control whether or not I get sick before I depart for McMurdo. I cannot change my circumstances. I can only surrender, yielding my rights of ownership, yielding control, giving up the right of deciding what is best for me or my possessions. I belong to him. My home belongs to him. My car belongs to him. My sailboat belongs to him. It all belongs to him, and he alone has the power of deciding how to use it or even dispose of it. I say again, he alone has the power of deciding how to use it or even dispose of it.

For days I had tried to discipline myself not to be anxious. But trying harder to overcome my anxiety did not work. Surrender did. Appalled, I confessed to the Father how I had attempted to control my situation with getting the job in Antarctica. Same with taking care of the sailboat before I left. I had tried to figure it out on my own instead of resting in the knowledge that the Father was the only owner of the vessel. He alone had the power of deciding what was best and how to dispose of it if necessary. If he didn't want to sell it, it wouldn't sell. If he wanted to store it, he would store it. It was not my decision to make. So I waited for him to tell me what he wanted me to do with his things.

Further, the Bible says, "The Lord is at hand." He is not some faraway God, unconcerned with our day-to-day lives. He is near. He is with us. The one who owns all things and has the authority to decide what is best is close. He is aware. It is not as if he is somehow preoccupied somewhere far away in the universe. He is here! With us!

According to this passage, my sole responsibility is to bring all my requests to the Father, by prayer and supplication, with thanksgiving. I spent an hour talking with the Father, surrendering anew and afresh, letting go of my desire to control, yielding fully, finally resting in his embrace. My prayer had little to do with going to Antarctica and even less to do with a sailboat. It had everything to do with emptying my heart. The one thing that truly matters to the Father. My heart.

For me, the key to overcoming anxiety is not trying harder. It is surrender. And so I do not ask for relief; I ask for conformity. The Father pulls, stretches, and slowly conforms me to the image of his son Jesus. Jesus, the son who trusted his Father fully even to the point of laying down his life. When we are aware of the presence of the Lord with us, we do not need to be anxious about anything. He is at hand. He is near. He is with us. Because of that, we let go of our anxious thoughts.

At that moment, the peace of God, which surpasses all understanding, guards our hearts and our minds in Christ Jesus. When I surrendered control to the Father, I found a fresh perspective and peace. Options for storing the boat became clear, negating the pressure to make a quick sale before departure. Peace settled in where anxiety had ruled. And most importantly, the Father realigned my heart with his.

Little did I know how quickly circumstances in my world would change.

The Peace that Guards Us

Within days, the sailboat sold. It was an immense relief to know I had taken care of this before departing for Antarctica. I celebrated this milestone.

That's the good news. Now for the bad news.

A few days later, I received an email from my supervisor in Antarctica. The subject line read, "Unfortunate News." Cautiously, I opened the email. The National Science Foundation (NSF) oversees the research and work at McMurdo, Antarctica. Due to the escalating pandemic, they decided to cut back the scale of work at McMurdo that season. Unfortunately, as a result, my position was eliminated. That's right. Downsized. Cut. Gone. Crickets chirping. I was back in alternate status. If anything opened up, they would let me know.

I sat there on the couch, trying to process the message, and reread the email on my cell phone. And I smiled. Yes, I actually smiled. And here is where it gets interesting.

You would imagine I would be disappointed, sad, bummed out. But I was not. I sat there smiling, completely content, not a care in the world, not the least bit disappointed. I began to wonder if I was mentally okay. Had I finally lost my mind? Had the stress become so great that I had completely lost it?

I had the most astounding peace. I do not have words to describe it. No worry. No anxiety. Just complete, utter peace, satisfied, full of joy. Not a care in the world.

And that is when the lesson I recently learned came back to my mind. Ah, yes, the Lord is at hand. Do not be anxious. Surrender everything to the Father. And the peace of God, which is beyond all understanding, will guard your heart and your mind.

There it was! I was experiencing the peace of God that is beyond understanding! It was guarding me, protecting my heart, defending my mind. I was stunned. I had never experienced anything like it. Honestly, I kept waiting for the other shoe to fall. Surely dismay would follow. But peace remained, anchoring me, filling me, washing over me.

Child's Toys

I settled in to spend a few moments talking about the situation with the Father. Then, in my mind, I saw myself sitting on his lap, on his left knee. His arm was around me, his hand resting on my leg. I craned my neck and looked down over the side of his leg. There, on the floor below at his feet, was a tiny toy sailboat lying on its side. Nearby, to the right of the sailboat, was a small toy home. Then, just further away, I saw a child-sized puzzle, partially finished, the three or four remaining pieces scattered about the edges. On the face of the puzzle was the continent of Antarctica, nearly complete.

In that beautiful moment, I saw my life from the perspective of the lap of God, and it changed everything. My toys, the things I highly value in my childlike mind, lay scattered at his feet. There on his lap, none of them mattered in the least. His embrace overwhelmed me. His love filled me to the full. I sat there looking at my toys and realized there is no comparison to the feeling I get when I am with the Father. Nothing even comes close. I sat there on his lap, resting in his peace, willing to set aside my toys for the joy of being with the Father, who loves me so profoundly.

I don't recall ever experiencing peace like this in my life. It was a big moment, one I will long remember. I suspect the path to this overwhelming peace begins with surrender. I believe the moments of surrender I experienced a few weeks before made possible the peace I enjoyed now. For peace is unlikely while we cling to our toys, our problems, and our circumstances.

Further, the peace of God is not something we generate through will or effort. It is something given to us by the Father. It is the peace *of* or *from* God. Some reading this will think, "Wow, look how Tim responded." But that implies I am somehow willing myself to have peace. That is not true! No, it is the supernatural peace of God at work. His peace is doing the heavy lifting.

The Bible says the peace of God guards us. In the original language, it is a military term. His peace sets up a perimeter around us like a special forces team with guns drawn, defending against anything that would discourage, defeat, or cause anxiety from affecting our hearts and our minds. We merely sit there in the middle, surrendered to the Father's embrace, surrounded by his peace. His peace guards our hearts, that place of emotion and feeling. And it guards our minds, that place of intellect and thought. Ironically, the Bible says the peace of God is beyond understanding. And even though we cannot comprehend it, we experience it fully in our hearts and minds.

The Bible says when we are aware the owner of our lives and toys is near, we have no reason to be anxious about anything. We bring all our requests to our loving Father by prayer with thanksgiving. We crawl upon his lap to share our wants and needs with him. Then, the peace of God, which is beyond comprehension, guards our hearts and minds in Christ Jesus. The result of all this is that his peace protects us! Imagine. All our anxieties are vanquished. We rest in his care.

The Lord is at hand. We rest in his embrace.

Even to this day, when I go into a home where it's clearly a loving home, where the kids are happy and there's good food, and it's warm and cozy, I always feel this thing like wow, like amazing, like I sort of want to be adopted by them immediately. But I'm 45 years old and so that's not appropriate at this age.

—Dr. Andrew Huberman
Neuroscientist

Chapter 15

Grieving What Was Lost

One morning I felt a profound sadness while looking back on my life. Tears brimmed my eyes when I considered how different my life could have been if I had learned these truths sooner. I was grateful to see redeeming value in my experiences, bringing others to an awareness so they too can find healing. But there was also sadness. A sense of mourning over what could have been. A picking at old scabs, hoping to find bright pink, baby smooth, newly formed skin beneath, only to discover healing is still needed. And now there was a trace of blood to deal with as well.

I sat rehearsing failures, moments locked in time that could have changed the trajectory of my life if only I had responded differently. I grieved over painful moments in my childhood. But moments of childhood trauma represent only a fraction of time in the course of my life. My compensating behavior fills the gap between my childhood and today. Those moments are the moments I grieve the most. I grieve the loss of what could have been if only I had known what it meant to sit upon the lap of

God, to experience the love of the Father and his healing touch. How altered my life could have been.

One time, as a young adult, a loving friend sat down with me after church. She sat in the row behind me, leaning onto the row I occupied. I sat kitty-corner to her with my arm over the back of the chair, leaning back into the conversation. The room was mostly empty as we talked, the congregation having exited from the service, heading for coffee and conversation in the lobby. She shared how concerned she was. It appeared to her I might be repeating unhealthy patterns in a relationship with a friend. I listened carefully to her words, but I believed this relationship was different. I tried to persuade her I was doing well. At the moment, I couldn't see the truth she so graciously offered to me. I wasn't trying to hide anything. I simply couldn't see reality. Looking back, her kindness and thoughtfulness in attempting to set me aright humbles me. I admire her for her bravery. It was just that at that moment, I couldn't see it. I genuinely felt I was right. Now I realize I was wrong. The fact I still remember the conversation today shows how deeply her words imprinted my mind.

In the following months, the relationship I was in at the time repeated the same unhealthy pattern as all the relationships before it. I felt loved, and the feeling was addicting. I lost my sense of self and morphed into what I thought I needed to be to continue to get my fix. I rescued. I served selflessly. I was self-deprecating, desperate to get another fix of the feeling that made me feel valued, validated. On the surface, it looked so godly, so spiritual. But it was far from it.

And so I wonder what could have been. How different my life could have been if I had found the lap of the Father sooner. And that is okay. It is part of the grieving process. We grieve our losses. We cry. We remember. In the process, we let go. We surrender. We confirm our footing is solid, and though the path may be steep, it is secure to move forward.

Grieving is a necessary step in our journey. It is a natural step in the process of forgiving others and forgiving ourselves. We forgive others for harm brought upon us. And we forgive ourselves for our part in our failures. But we grieve with an understanding of our position as sons and daughters of the Father God. This is essential. We grieve with an understanding of the hope we have as his children.

That morning, as I sat and meditated on my place with the Father, I saw myself sitting on his lap, leaning back onto his chest. I was sad, considering my past. But it was okay. I was sitting with the Father. He was holding me. It was from the place of wholeness and security that I viewed the days from long ago as if looking out over a vast, distant field. I was safe. He had healed me. He held me securely. I no longer live in the past, but I can still grieve the past as needed. I choose not to dwell on my mistakes. I choose to grieve them and then move on.

The Bible says, "the kind of sorrow God wants us to experience leads us away from sin and results in salvation. There's no regret for that kind of sorrow. But worldly sorrow, which lacks repentance, results in spiritual death."

There is godly grief and worldly grief. One leads to positive change; the other leads to spiritual death. The difference between the two is repentance. The helpful kind of grief is the kind that leads us to turn away from past behaviors, embracing a new way of living in an intimate relationship with the Father. This is the kind of grief we welcome. Without turning away from past behaviors, our grief only leads to depression and anxiety because there is no expectation of change. It is only a feeling of sorrow leading to more despair. It is hopeless grief or grief without hope.

The Bible says, "there is a time to cry and a time to laugh, a time to grieve and a time to dance." How we love to laugh. How we love to dance. But after the celebration, the wonder, the ecstasy of how profoundly our lives are filled on the lap of the Father, after we are exhausted from the adrenaline of reaching the height of the mountain, comes a stillness. We settle in, spent from joy. And it is in the stillness that we look back, and we grieve. Sorrow and joy mingled together. Laughter and crying. Grieving and dancing. Both are necessary. For even as we grieve, we look forward. The Father doesn't leave us to focus on what we lost in our journey. No, he renews. He heals.

We crest the hill to see a splendid valley laid out below us. Green hills spill into crooked ravines where pure, clean water flows. He leads us beside still waters. He restores us. He renews our strength. And as we gingerly find our footing on the path before us, we discover we can no longer see the way where we have traveled. It is too far over the crest behind us. We can remember, but we no longer live there. What is past has passed. And even the memories fade with time.

Grieving is a necessary part of healing. It is a steppingstone on the path to wholeness, one natural yet painful step in our journey with the Father. Nevertheless, it is necessary to move forward. We cannot circumvent this step. In the process of grieving, we let go of regrets. We grieve lost expectations of childhood. We grieve choices we made as we tried to fill the void, as we stumbled along the way. We accept our humanity as we tumble onto the lap of God.

A Place of Hope

David, the shepherd king of Israel, understood this. He wrote many of the song lyrics and poems collected in the book of Psalms in the Bible. He is my favorite biblical character because of his creative personality and his love for the Father. But I also admire his transparency and willingness to reveal his weaknesses and failures.

Sometimes we forget David grew up in a highly dysfunctional family. His father, Jesse, blatantly showed favor to David's brothers. When God sent the prophet Samuel to anoint one of Jesse's sons as the new king of Israel, Jesse presented each of David's brothers while leaving David in the field to tend the sheep. Only after Samuel asked if there were any other sons did Jesse reluctantly admit there was one more, one son out in the field tending sheep. And tending sheep was pretty much the lowest job on the farm.

If this was not enough, his siblings verbally abused David. They belittled him. They assumed the worst of his intentions when he brought food to them on the battlefield. His home life was a dysfunctional mess.

David's relationships were a mess as well. As an adult, he had an affair with a married woman. Then, as if that was not enough, he had her husband murdered in an attempt to cover it up.

Yet, despite his humanity, despite failure after failure, despite dysfunctional relationships, in spite of many attempts to fill a void from his childhood, the Bible says David was a man after God's own heart. Yes, all this mess, yet the Father finds a way to connect with him in an intimate relationship.

When I read David's writings, a theme of grieving surfaces. Often, he wrote of his grief and sorrow. In one psalm, he wrote, "The Lord is close to the brokenhearted; he rescues those whose spirits are crushed." David understood what it meant to be brokenhearted. He understood the crushing ache of a lost expectation. He understood failure and his humanity. He understood how choices for which he alone was responsible had broken him. He deeply grieved his own sinful choices. After the affair, he cried out to God in heartfelt repentance. He wrote, "The sacrifices of God are a broken spirit; a broken and contrite heart, O God, you will not despise."

We grieve hurtful experiences. We also grieve moments when we hurt others. In both cases, the Father God is near. He knows. He understands. He is aware. But he is also near. He does not leave us in our grief. He does not abandon us in our mess. He does not withdraw his love from us. Instead, he draws us close to himself upon his lap, holding us tightly. He does not leave us alone to deal with our grief. No, he pulls us in, drawing us close.

We do not grieve alone. The Father grieves with us. He understands our weaknesses. He remembers he formed us from the dust at the moment of creation.

Of all the psalms David wrote, one stanza, in particular, is a personal favorite. It is from Psalm 103:

> The Lord is merciful and gracious, slow to anger
>   and abounding in steadfast love.
> He will not always chide, nor will he keep his
>   anger forever.
> He does not deal with us according to our sins, nor
>   repay us according to our iniquities.
> For as high as the heavens are above the earth, so
>   great is his steadfast love toward those who
>   fear him;
> as far as the east is from the west, so far does he
>   remove our transgressions from us.
> As a father shows compassion to his children, so
>   the Lord shows compassion to those who
>   fear him.
> For he knows our frame; he remembers that we
>   are dust.

Personally, I need a father like that. I relish his mercy and grace, his slowness to anger and abounding, steadfast love. His love for me is so vast; he chooses not to deal with me as I deserve. He shows me unbounded compassion. He will never abandon me. He knows every wrong choice I have made, every flaw in my frame, and yet remembers that he formed me from the dust. He knows my DNA and loves me anyway.

In the stillness, he lifts me onto his lap. He strokes my back, tension easing. I grieve my losses while clinging to his hand.

From working with all the celebrities I've worked with, I found that sometimes the people that are the most famous are the most lonely.

—Katherine Brooks
Screenwriter

Chapter 16

Receiving and Giving Grace

The sins of my youth haunt me. One morning, while spending time with the Father, I caught myself reviewing in my mind a porn video I saw years ago. It was on auto play before I realized I had rewatched it in my mind for a few moments. It was shocking how easily it slipped into my stream of thought, even as I was trying to focus on my relationship with the Father. Once I realized what was happening, I shut it down. But it was a reminder of terrible choices I have made. It was a reminder of how badly I have blown it in the past, and a clue of how much grace the Father has given to me through the years.

I am overwhelmed when I consider the depth of his grace. Authors have written entire volumes on this singular word. *Grace*. I do not claim to understand it fully, even as I claim to have received it. Yet, somehow, the Father gives me grace when I sin. It is a sense that while he is aware of my sin, he looks at the balance sheet and sees Jesus already paid in full the payment for my sin. Grace is given. I do not receive the penalty for my sin because it has already been paid on my behalf through the death of his Son on the cross.

The remarkable aspect of grace is how frequently I have received it. It is not a one-time event. I have blown it so many times. To this day, I still blow it. Yet he continues to give me grace. So again, it is not as if there is no consequence for my sin; it is just that there is no penalty, no harsh judgment. Discipline? Yes. Hit in anger for my actions? No. Just grace. Pure grace.

Undeserved Grace

We do not deserve the Father's grace, and we cannot earn grace. Instead, the Father freely gives it to us. We receive it despite our behavior. It is essential to understand this truth. Without an understanding of our sin and the depth of grace we have received, we are unable to give grace to others. Giving grace to others begins with an understanding of the grace we have already received.

I give grace to others not because they deserve it but because it is the character of the Spirit of the Father within me to give grace to others. When the Spirit is living within me, his character seeps out of me. So yes, in my flesh, I am not giving grace to anyone. But when I am filled with the Spirit, experiencing the rush of his grace filling me to the full, then out of the overflow of his grace, I give it to others. Often, when we are unable to give grace to others, there is an unawareness of our own need for grace for ourselves.

An important side note here. Giving grace, forgiveness, or mercy does not alleviate the consequences of someone's actions. It merely frees me from any malice toward the person who hurt me. It opens the door to be able to love the offender despite their sin. For example, if someone commits murder, they can receive grace and forgiveness from the offended family members while still serving time in prison. They receive grace but still have to deal with the consequence of their offense.

I understand giving grace seems unnatural. To love someone who has profoundly hurt us seems unthinkable. We may still need to set healthy boundaries between ourselves and someone who hurts us, but we can still love them. This concept is difficult for some to grasp.

The Father gives us grace, not because we deserve it, but because it is his character to do so. Therefore, with the Spirit of the Father within us we give grace to others, not because they deserve it, but because it is the character of the Father within us to do so. This fundamental principle applies to many aspects of our lives. This core value sets us free to love, extend grace, mercy, and forgiveness, even when the offending party doesn't deserve it. For many, the offending party never acknowledges their offense. Never.

We are all unperfect people. None of us are without guilt. But all of us receive grace in our time of need. The Bible says when sin increases, grace abounds all the more. Extravagant offenses need extravagant grace. Gratefully, in the Father God's economy, this is how grace works. I need this kind of grace.

I learned this principle in a round-about way. At the time, the Father was working in my life to teach me how to be generous. Generosity was the theme of many conversations with him. At the time, I was a stingy person. I was making slow progress and learning to be generous was often on my mind. It all came to a head at a restaurant in the Detroit airport.

I had time for dinner while waiting for a flight. I settled into a booth at the restaurant and ordered. My server brought my meal and a glass of ice water. All was well. Unfortunately, that was the last time I saw my server for some time. I devoured the spicy burger and fries. My water was gone. Even the ice had melted. With every bite, I was getting more thirsty. I looked around the restaurant, searching for my server. I couldn't find her. My throat was dry. My blood pressure started to rise.

I was becoming more frustrated by the minute. All I wanted was a refill. Was that too much to ask? Finally, I saw her and flagged her down. She returned with a pitcher of lukewarm water, filled my glass, and walked away. She didn't put any ice in my glass. Nothing. Just a glass of warm water. I sat there staring at the glass as she walked away. By this point, I was so thirsty I begrudgingly drank some of the water just to relieve my parched throat. I was fuming. The service was horrible. I did not deserve such callous treatment. I was a paying customer!

Finally, it came time to pay the bill, which meant it was also time to calculate a tip. What to do? Should I send a strong message about the lousy service and leave a measly little tip? I usually tip twenty percent. But this service deserved five percent, if that.

I sat there, dirty dishes in front of me, a nearly full glass of warm water table center, and heard the voice of the Father speaking to me. "Tim," he said, "I am generous to you, not because you deserve it, but because it is my character to do so. Therefore, with my Spirit within you, you can be generous to others, not because they deserve it, but because it is your character to do so." I sat there stunned, realizing the Father had set the whole scenario in place to teach me this simple but important lesson. My actions, in regard to others, are not dependent on the other person deserving it. My character determines my actions. Period. Let that sink in. Look at how this applies to our lives.

I give grace to others, not because they deserve it, but because it is my character to do so.

I forgive others, not because they deserve it, but because it is my character to do so.

I love others, not because they deserve it, but because it is my character to do so.

Our character determines our actions. Someone else's

actions do not determine our response. As difficult as it may seem, we give grace to those who have hurt us, not because they deserve it, but because it is our character to do so. It doesn't free them from any responsibility for their actions. No. It frees us! We are free to live our lives to the full without needing someone to own what they have done. We are free to love, to laugh, to live with no regard for someone else's behavior. This simple truth sets us free!

Further, when we do not give grace, we assume we are a competent judge and jury for another person's behavior. I could assume my server didn't care about me. I could assume she was a lazy person. I could assume she was incompetent. But what if that morning, her husband told her he was having an affair and was leaving her for the other woman? What if she could hardly show up for work that day because the news had devastated her world? What if her mind was reeling, trying to figure out what she was going to do after her shift finally ended? Who am I to know what was going on in her world that day? Then I show up and treat her poorly because she somehow missed filling my glass with cold water. Oh, and by the way, I claim to be a follower of Jesus. Yes, the same Jesus who loved the most unfortunate, the sinners, the wretched. Yes, the same Jesus who loved *me* so much he died for *my* wretched sin so I could have a relationship with the Father. Yet, I claim to receive grace from the Father and then hoard it to myself. It is inconceivable.

Giving grace has little to do with the other person. It has everything to do with understanding our relationship with our Father.

The Bible says we have all received "grace upon grace." I love that phrase. To take it one step further, since we have received grace upon grace, let us give grace upon grace out of the grace we have received. Give grace out of the abundance of grace received.

Oh, and in case you're wondering, I left a twenty percent tip.

Flinch

Even as we learn to give grace, mercy, and forgiveness, we find in ourselves an instinctive pattern to expect more harm. We unconsciously expect to be hurt again, so we build defensive habits to protect ourselves. Undoing this may take time.

My brother's family adopted a shelter dog. They named him Prince. Prince is a small mixed breed with the face of a Chihuahua and the body of a Beagle or a Jack Russell Terrier. He has a tan coat and will play fetch until you are exhausted. Just mention the word "ball," and his body will tremble while his face lights up with pure joy. I have always loved lap dogs, and Prince is the perfect size to fill your lap.

The first time I met Prince, I wanted to show the little guy how much I loved him, so I reached down to pet him on his head. He flinched. He squinted his eyes closed and lowered his head, ears flattening and tail slightly tucked, cowering away from me. All because I extended my open hand toward him. I looked at my brother to see if he had noticed, and he nodded his head in agreement at the observation. Someone had hurt Prince in his past. The signs were obvious.

We all loved the little guy. While visiting my brother's family, I would hold Prince on my lap for extended sessions. I stroked his back, massaged his shoulders, and bonded with him. While he lay on my lap, I rested my hand on him, letting him know I was near.

It took a long time for Prince to trust his new family. But over time, the flinch faded from view. The last time I visited, it was gone entirely. I smiled as I reached down to pet him, and there was no evidence of a flinch. Prince had found a safe, loving home and had found healing from his past.

In a lot of ways, I am like Prince. I know what it means to flinch. I did it for years while recovering. It is not a physical flinch. It is an emotional flinch. I flinched whenever someone began to show affection toward me. I instinctively raised my guard. This pattern was especially evident with a father or authority figure. It was a manner of looking at someone trying to discern if I could trust them or not. The assumption was that I could not. They would have to prove it. And they would have to prove it over and over and over again before I would reach a place where I did not flinch in the relationship. That would take years.

Ironically, God built flinching into our DNA. It is a protective mechanism. It is helpful in situations with genuine peril. But the reality is sometimes we flinch when it is unnecessary. Just like Prince flinched when I first met him and attempted to love on him, sometimes we flinch when others try to love on us. We assume offense, even when none is intended. This flinch, in turn, causes harm in our relationships. I hurt others when I presume they might hurt me. In the split second of interaction, I judge motives and assume the worst. I know this is not fair to the other party. But it is an unfortunate by-product of living in a sin-marred world.

Now imagine how I carried this into my relationship with the Father God. Mentally, I understood he loved me. I read in the Bible how he gave his Son to pay the penalty for my sin so he could have a relationship with me. I understood the Father had adopted me into the family of God. But understanding this in a cognitive sense didn't magically erase the flinch I had practiced for years.

The idea of trusting the Father God took me many years to process. I am still growing in this area. Again and again, it surfaces as a theme of my conversations with him. It saddens me to consider how this issue walks with me on nearly every step of my journey. I suspect it took root in my childhood, growing and blossoming along the way, a poisonous lack of trust in the Father's kindness, goodness, faithfulness, and love. It chokes anything of beauty that remains.

Sitting on the lap of God transformed this lack of trust. The more time I spent with him, the safer I felt. I sat on his lap for hours on end, learning to enjoy his presence. He wanted nothing from me but my presence with him. He didn't make me prove my love. He understood every wound I had received. He understood my flinch. He took no offense but instead loved me all the more, tracing his finger down my scars, resting his hand upon my shoulder as I sat with him. The longer I stayed in his presence, the more I came to trust him. Little by little, I let my guard down. Little by little, my flinch faded away.

Again, the Bible says the Father God knows how he made us. He remembers he created us out of the dust of the earth. He understands why we respond the way we do. He knows every wound we have received, ones we hide from others, held deeply in the darkest corners of our hearts. He knows them all. And his love is patient and kind.

This is why we need grace from others. This is why we need to give grace to ourselves. And this is why we all need grace from the Father. We relish his grace, his forgiveness, his love. If only we could stay in that simple place. But eventually, the Father will test us to see what we have learned.

This, I would find, would be the greatest challenge in my journey with him.

Often, when we describe loneliness, I think what we're saying is that when I'm on my own, I feel bad about myself, I feel like I'm not loved enough. I feel like I'm not good enough.

—Russell Brand
Comedian, actor, and radio host

Chapter 17

The Wilderness of Testing

In the early days of my discovering the lap of God, I still attempted to meet my needs on my own. I was desperate. I keenly felt the sense of emptiness inside, the longing for something more, a feeling of being disconnected. It was an unwanted companion, chatting endlessly, droning on, white noise in the background of my life. I had no understanding it was part of my DNA. I did not realize the Father God intended to fill that place he created within me. So, naturally, I did everything I could to fill it, always with unfortunate conclusions. I do not fault myself for trying. It was instinctive. We feel pain, and we recoil. It is how God designed us. Attempting to fill the Father-shaped hole, the Universal Ache, is only natural as well. We feel it deep within, and we try to fill it. We try anything. And who can blame us?

I also did not understand how our enemy works to prevent the Father from having a relationship with us. If you ever feel like the world is against you, you may be right. We have an enemy who hates the Father. His goal is to prevent the Father from having a relationship with us. He loves it when we try to fill the void apart from the Father. In his twisted mind, he has no interest in us discovering the love of the Father. So he presents a myriad of options to us while failing to tell us none will satisfy. Even as you read these words, the enemy will likely try to distract you from this truth. Chaos is likely to erupt. Brace for it. Indeed, he does not want us to understand these truths.

During this season in my life, chaos indeed erupted. I had an accident with my sailboat and had to deal with the subsequent repairs. The marina repairing the boat was two hours and forty-five minutes from home, complicating matters. I worked full-time in construction, remodeling homes to raise funds for the rudder repair. I spent evenings preparing my home for the tourist rental market as I moved to live aboard the sailboat. I tried to maintain the ministry. I worked six days a week, ten to twelve hours a day, for almost five months. In the middle of all this, Hurricane Irma hit, a category three hurricane whose eyewall came within twenty miles of my home. I dealt with issues related to the storm for days before and after the chaos. Ministry work felt like it was on autopilot. The pace of life exhausted me physically, spiritually, and emotionally.

I struggled to maintain my relationship with the Father. I spent time reading the Bible, but it felt dry and uninspired. I talked with the Father about it, but even those conversations felt empty.

During this time, I also experienced lustful thoughts far beyond typical temptations. I'm used to the usual thoughts we all have as guys, but this was different. I mentioned to several friends how shocking these thoughts were. In my whole life, I don't think I've ever before entertained such temptations. The temptation was so strong that for a moment, I even considered walking away from the ministry to fulfill it. The next moment I had clarity and shuddered to think I would even consider such things. It frightened me I could even think that way.

In all, those months felt different from anything I had ever experienced in my relationship with the Father. Something was going on, but I was not sure what it was. I plodded on in my relationship with the Father but struggled to find intimacy with him.

Finally, in the midst of all this, I heard the still small voice of the Father. "Tim," he said, "you need to be extremely careful. This season in your life is not just the Valley of Wait. I have led you to the Wilderness of Testing." It was a quiet word to my spirit, but it felt like he shouted it to me. At that moment, I saw the context of what had transpired over the past months. Suddenly, a light turned on, and the context of what I had been dealing with was finally clear.

Oddly, I was greatly encouraged.

The Wilderness of Testing

We see this type of testing when the enemy approached Jesus in the wilderness after Jesus had fasted for forty days. I mentioned this story earlier when we discovered our identity as sons and daughters of the Father. That morning, when I heard the Father speaking so clearly to me, I was reminded of this story. So I looked it up to get a better understanding of the context. I was stunned by what I found.

As we grow in our understanding of what it means to have an intimate relationship with the Father, at some point, he likely will test us to see what we have learned and what lessons we need to take again. Within the story of the temptation of Jesus, I discovered three key areas where the Father was testing me to see what I had learned. Physically, spiritually, and emotionally, I was being tested. Would I pass the test?

The first thing I noticed in the story was how the Holy Spirit led Jesus to the wilderness for this testing. It was not accidental he was in this place. God led him there. It was intentional. It was for a purpose. Jesus followed the leading of the Holy Spirit into the wilderness. Understanding this gave a sense of purpose to all I had experienced over the past six months. There was a reason, even if I did not yet know what it was. It was not merely a season of waiting.

Will We Meet Our Needs on Our Own?

Remember how the enemy tried to question Jesus' identity? We discussed earlier how the enemy begins with this attack. But the story continues. The Bible says Jesus had completed his fast and he was hungry. And what does the enemy say? "If you are the Son of God, command these stones to become loaves of bread." On the surface, this temptation seems like no big deal. Jesus could speak a word, and a stone would miraculously become a steaming hot loaf of homemade bread. Why not? If you're hungry and you can meet the need, why wouldn't you?

Further, our enemy understands our needs better than we do. So he struck where he suspected Jesus had the greatest need. "Go ahead," he whispers, "turn these stones into bread. You're hungry. You deserve it."

This moment gives us a small clue of how our enemy tends to strike. The enemy will likely attack in the area where our felt needs are most significant. He understands our built-in need to fill the Father-shaped hole better than we do. So he appeals to this area of our lives. "Go ahead," he says, "I know you feel empty inside. I understand. Here, have another drink." Or "Here, have another look at that porn site." Or "Here, have another cookie." He will offer us anything except the relationship with the Father. How clever. And we fall for it over and over again. At least, I did.

Notice also this was a legitimate need. Jesus was hungry.

This core enticement is the temptation to meet a legitimate need in an illegitimate way. It is okay to be hungry. That is normal. It is okay to experience a pang of hunger to be loved by the Father. That is also normal. The Father designed us this way. But meet the legitimate need through the Father! Let him meet the need with his love. We need to let him fill us with his love instead of trying to fill the void with porn, food, work, success, social media, or any other option. Don't fall to this base temptation by our enemy!

This temptation may explain the overwhelming lustful thoughts I experienced. It is the one area of my life I struggled with the most. On a regular day, I want to fulfill the typical physical desires God created within me. But when I am tired and "hungry," the temptation is more challenging to resist.

Gratefully, Jesus responded to the first temptation with clarity as an example for us to follow. He replied, "It is written, 'Man shall not live by bread alone, but by every word that comes from the mouth of God.'"

Significantly, Jesus refuted the enemy with Scripture. Jesus quoted a passage in the Old Testament. In this passage, Moses was addressing the nation of Israel as they looked forward to the fulfillment of God's promise to give them the land. Here is what Moses said:

"He humbled you and let you hunger and fed you with manna, which you did not know, nor did your fathers know, that he might make you know that man does not live by bread alone, but man lives by every word that comes from the mouth of the Lord."

On the surface, this seems like an odd response for Jesus to make. The apparent solution to hunger is to eat bread. But Jesus knows we are more than physical beings. We are spiritual as well. We do not live by physical nurture alone, but by every word that comes from the mouth of the Father God. We need spiritual sustenance even more than physical sustenance. Unfortunately, the enemy tempts us to ignore the spiritual side of the coin. "You don't need the Father God. You have everything you need within you. You can do it! Just meet your needs in the way that feels right for you." But he never tells us it will never satisfy. That is the saddest aspect of this temptation. When we attempt to meet our needs apart from the Father, it never works.

Moses' words give a better understanding of the purposes of the test. Like a test given by a teacher at school, it reveals what we have learned or still need to learn. It exposes what is in our heart and expands our understanding of our relationship with the Father.

It is also significant to realize the Israelites were looking forward to the Promised Land. They had not yet taken possession of it. The path to the Promised Land for the Israelites led through the wilderness. Often, in our lives, the path to a promise leads through a wilderness of testing. Perhaps you can relate. We look forward to the promise of a life that is whole, filled with the love of the Father. But that promise may lead us through a wilderness. That is okay. We focus on what is to come, not on what has passed.

At its core, this temptation is one of the critical challenges of our fatherlessness. Because the Father-shaped hole manifests itself in the physical realm, we try to meet the need with physical realm solutions. But it never works. As we have seen, fatherlessness is a spiritual condition. The love of the Father God is the only thing that can fill it. We cannot live by bread alone. We live by every word that comes from the Father God.

The enemy will likely strike in the area where our felt needs are most significant. But he is only beginning. He has more up his sleeve. Two more tests remained, as I was about to find out.

I was a millionaire, I had beautiful women in my life, I had cars, a house, an incredible solid-gold career, and a future, yet on a daily basis I wanted to commit suicide.

—Eric Clapton
Singer

Chapter 18

Asking the Hard Questions

Understanding the enemy tends to attack in an area of felt need was helpful. But the sexual temptation was only a small part of a larger protracted trial. Discouragement, physical and mental exhaustion, and financial stress were significant aspects of life throughout this season. As I mentioned earlier, I call this overall season The Wilderness of Testing. It is a season explicitly designed by God to test us, to see what we have learned.

Earlier I also mentioned how difficult it was for me to trust the Father God. I shared how he took me layer by layer in my life to expose areas where I needed to trust him fully. I would love to say I have never had an issue trusting him since that time. But it would be a lie. Trusting him is one of the critical areas in which I continue to grow. I can explain my lack of trust because of experiences in my past, but the Father God never accepts this excuse.

When I looked at the story of the temptation of Jesus in the wilderness, the first temptation seemed to be in the physical realm. This I painfully understood. The next temptation seemed to be in the spiritual realm, in the area of trusting God. Is he alone enough?

Will We Trust the Father?

The Bible says that after the first temptation, then the devil took Jesus to Jerusalem and set him high on top of the Temple. As they surveyed the city around them, he said, "If you are the Son of God, throw yourself down, for it is written, 'He will command his angels concerning you,' and 'On their hands they will bear you up, lest you strike your foot against a stone.'"

Another pause as Jesus considered his words. Finally, Jesus replied, "Again it is written, 'You shall not put the Lord your God to the test.'"

It is helpful for us to look deeper into this conversation between the enemy and Jesus. Once again, the enemy begins his attack by questioning Jesus' identity. He says, "If you are the Son of God." He used this phrase in the first temptation. It is significant he uses this line again. Why? Remember, our enemy wants to destroy the Father's relationship with us. If our enemy can get us to question our identity as sons and daughters of the Father God, then that relationship is in grave danger. Therefore, we must carefully guard our identity.

Then, from the pinnacle of the Temple, the devil tells Jesus to throw himself down. "After all," he sneers, "the Bible says God will rescue you. So why not make him prove it? You're his son, right?

Once again, Jesus rebukes the enemy with Scripture. "Again it is written, 'You shall not put the Lord your God to the test.'"

Now, if you are like me, I've read this passage before and glossed right over what Jesus just said. This time, as I looked into this, I wondered what it meant to put God to the test. What was Jesus saying?

To understand what Jesus says, we need to look at the passage he references. First, Jesus refers to a passage in the Old Testament in which Moses was addressing the Israelite nation. In this passage, Moses says, "You shall not put the Lord your God to the test, as you tested him at Massah."

We're getting closer. Now we need to find out what happened at Massah. For this, we look to the story of how Moses led the nation of Israel out of Egypt. The Bible says as the people of Israel were traveling in the desert, they ran out of water. Thirst overwhelmed them. There were about six hundred thousand men on foot, besides women and children. Hot, tired, exhausted, lips cracking in the heat, it wasn't long before tensions flared. They quarreled with Moses. "Give us water to drink," they angrily demanded.

Moses shot back, "Why do you quarrel with me? Why do you test the Lord?"

In reality, Moses was as frustrated as they were. He cried out to God, "What shall I do with this people? They are almost ready to stone me."

Here, again, we see the patience of the Father God, for the Father was kind to Moses and kind to the children of Israel. God miraculously provided water to flow out of a rock, and all the people had fresh water to drink. And the Bible says Moses "called the name of the place Massah and Meribah, because of the quarreling of the people of Israel, and because they tested the Lord by saying, 'Is the Lord among us or not?'"

The Hebrew word for "tested" in this passage expresses the idea of putting the Father to the test to make him prove himself. It connects with the idea of doubting God. It is a test born out of doubt instead of faith.

The Israelites were thirsty by design. God led them to that place. In their discomfort, they complained to one another. They complained to Moses. It seems they spoke to everyone but the

Father. They tested the Lord by saying in effect, "Is the Lord among us or not? Then he should prove it."

The Father God tests us to see where we are in our relationship with him, but it is not okay for you and me to test the Father to prove how he feels in his relationship with us. He never changes. His love is a constant burning flame. It is our love for him that flickers. The irony is we tend to test God when he is testing us. He allows trials in our lives to see what we have learned in our relationship with him, but instead of trusting him, we tend to test him. As a result, we doubt his love and care. Are you here? Do you love me? Can I trust you? Are you loving or not?

Don't do it. Do not test the Father. Instead of testing him, trust him. Trust him even when it does not make sense. Choose to love the Father God rather than trying to understand him. This truth is perhaps the greatest lesson I've learned: it is better to love the Father than to try to understand him. He is entirely in control.

Herein lies a bomb buried in the road before us. Those who have experienced childhood trauma or abandonment in a father-child relationship naturally project a lack of trust in one's human father onto a relationship with the Father God. I certainly did. In the early days of my relationship with the Father God, I did not trust him. Trusting him was the furthest thing from my mind. At the time, I was blind to this truth. It took a long time before I could hesitantly let go. This lack of trust is why the process of surrendering my life to him took so long. I had to learn he was trustworthy. I had to learn it in my heart, not just in my head.

Gratefully, the Father understands. He is aware of our inability to trust him. So he proves he is trustworthy over and over again. He is worthy of being trusted. So he does not scold us, but he also will not let us stay where we are.

Is the Father God trustworthy? Ultimately, this is the question at the heart of this temptation. May we pass the test! May we rise and say, "I will trust the Father even when it does not make sense."

The first temptation of Jesus seems to be in the physical realm. Will we meet legitimate human needs apart from our relationship with the Father? The second temptation appears to be in the spiritual realm. Is the Father God enough? Will we trust him even when it does not make sense?

The final temptation seems to be in the area of our emotions. This temptation would be the most difficult one for me to address.

Will We Let Go of Unhealthy Desires?

In this closing scene of the temptation of Jesus, Satan goes for broke. He takes Jesus to the top of a high mountain and, with a sweeping gesture, shows Jesus all the kingdoms of the world and their glory. "I'll give you more than you can imagine," he whispers. "All you have to do is to trust me. Worship me. You don't need God. I'll give you all this glory and more."

When Satan offers Jesus the kingdoms of this world, I do not think he is referring to political kingdoms and nations. I suspect he is alluding to kingdoms of wealth, kingdoms of happiness, kingdoms of power, kingdoms of celebrity and fame, kingdoms of significance. These are the kingdoms of this earth. "Worship me," he says, "and I will give you all this." Note the passage says he offered Jesus "the kingdoms of this world *and their glory.*" He is not just offering him kingdoms; he is offering him their glory. This offer is key to understanding the basis of this temptation. It is the temptation to seek recognition for ourselves. It is the temptation to take our eyes off the Father God and to worship anything but him. It is the temptation for self-worship.

It is the temptation to seek our glory over the Father's. It is the temptation to seek wealth, happiness, power, celebrity, fame, significance, and the glory they represent.

The problem is none of these things ever satisfy. On the contrary, all leave us longing for more. Satan is a fraud. He offers glory but fails to mention it will never satisfy. We deeply feel the Universal Ache, the Father-shaped hole. We desperately try to fill it, but it always leaves us wanting more. More significance. More money. More toys. More followers on social media. More likes. More retweets. But none of it satisfies. None! Sadly, we've been duped. We bought the lie. We bowed down. And we are left empty.

The rise in social media has fueled this temptation, like pouring gasoline on a fire. In December 2017, a former Facebook executive shared how programmers intentionally developed the site to hook users by manipulating their emotional responses. "We curate our lives around this perceived sense of perfection because we get rewarded in these short-term signals: Hearts, likes, thumbs up," he said. "We conflate that with value, and we conflate it with truth. And instead, what it really is is fake, brittle popularity that's short-term and leaves you even more vacant and empty than before you did it."

We rate our success based on the number of Twitter followers or friends on Facebook. I've done it. Lately, I've questioned this. The answer led me to delete my Twitter account and severely cut back on my use of Facebook. How much of my social media use is ultimately to promote me? Do I use social media to feed an unhealthy desire for significance? These are the hard questions we need to ask ourselves.

The Search for Significance

Satan offers us significance. God offers us the opposite. Jesus said, "The greatest among you shall be your servant," and "Whoever humbles himself like this child is the greatest in the kingdom of heaven." Note he did not say the greatest among you will be a successful businessperson. He did not say the greatest among you will make the most money. He did not say the greatest among you will have the most significant social media following. He did not say the greatest among you will have the nicest home, drive the most expensive car, or live in the best neighborhood. He said the greatest would be your servant.

Even the disciples of Jesus dealt with this issue. The Bible says, "A dispute also arose among them, as to which of them was to be regarded as the greatest. And he [Jesus] said to them, 'The kings of the Gentiles exercise lordship over them, and those in authority over them are called benefactors. But not so with you. Rather, let the greatest among you become as the youngest, and the leader as one who serves.'"

If the disciples grappled with this issue, is it possible we do as well? I know I do.

My desire for significance is an ungodly motivating factor in my life. For most of my life, I have felt insignificant, worth little, etc. I have a natural sinful desire to counter those feelings. It crouches in the background of my life. For as long as I can remember, this desire has hidden behind the curtain on the stage, peeking out at me. I hear its whisper when I am speaking at an event.

Do I want to see the Father made great, or do I desire to see my kingdom made great? Is my desire a desire for significance? Even just a little? When I write a blog, do I hope it will go viral so people will see how perceptive I am? These are the difficult questions with which I wrestle in quiet moments alone with the Father.

Satan does his best to tempt Jesus away from God. But Jesus will have none of it. So he counters with a stunning command. "Be gone, Satan! You shall worship the Lord your God and him only shall you serve." Here he quotes yet another passage from Moses in the Bible. This time Moses was instructing the Israelites, "It is the LORD your God you shall fear. Him you shall serve and by his name you shall swear."

In the original language, the command "Be gone, Satan!" is the same statement Jesus says to his friend Peter on another occasion. Jesus had shared with the disciples that he was about to go to Jerusalem to lay down his life. Peter responded, "Far be it from you, Lord! This shall never happen to you." Jesus turned and said to Peter, "Get behind me *(be gone)*, Satan! You are a hindrance to me. For you are not setting your mind on the things of God, but on the things of man."

There it is. Did you catch it? "You are not setting your mind on the things of God, but on the things of man." He is referring to the kingdoms of this world, the things of man. It is the core temptation with which we all deal. We naturally set our minds on the things of this world – significance, wealth, happiness, prosperity, and on and on. But, gratefully, Jesus shows us a better way. He continues and explains how we are to live.

Then Jesus told his disciples, "If anyone would come after me, let him deny himself and take up his cross and follow me. For whoever would save his life will lose it, but whoever loses his life for my sake will find it."

Satan offers us the chance to be served. Jesus offers us servitude. Satan focuses on building wealth. Jesus focuses on our poverty. Satan offers fame and power. Jesus willingly set aside his power and submitted to death on a cross. Can you see the contrast?

God does not share his glory. The wise never try to capture it for themselves. It never ends well. His command to us is to love him with all our hearts, all our minds, all our strength. All, not most. All. He alone is worthy of our love and affection and service. We give ourselves to him alone.

While this may sound discouraging, what I found was incredibly encouraging. When we experience tests in this way, it frees us to address each of these issues. It frees us to rest in the Father's ability to meet all of our needs. It frees us to trust him without needing to understand him. It frees us to seek influence without significance. It frees us to pursue ministry without titles. It frees us to serve without needing someone's approval. Each area I addressed brought a brighter light of the Father's glory into my heart. And while the trial drained me of strength, it led me to a new place in my relationship with him.

We sit upon his lap. At that moment, he fills us to the full; our hunger met. With one hand, he holds us close to himself; with the other hand, he swirls the universe with his finger. His love, profound. His grace, an unending river flowing through us. We melt into his embrace with no thought of our importance. We are significant solely because we are his. And that is enough.

There are psychological needs that are just as valuable and important as physical needs. We know we have needs for nutrients. We have needs for water. We have needs that are psychological for all sorts of different things. Our communities are incredibly important. Love is incredibly important. Family is incredibly important.

—Joe Rogan
Comedian, UFC commentator, podcaster

Chapter 19

Discovering a New Family

Looking back on my failures humbles me. For most of my life, I struggled alone. I rarely spoke of the challenges I was facing, slogging my way through life, trying to fill the emptiness, failing again and again. I did the best I could, not understanding these truths I'm sharing with you now. Shame kept me isolated, alone, set apart. I did not know I was set apart by the Father God to be his son, to be held by him, to dwell with him, to be in his family.

For many years, I attended church on the weekends and was even in leadership behind the scenes. On Sunday, I would drive to church and make my way into the auditorium. Typically, around eight hundred attended our Sunday service. The service began and ended within an hour and a half. It began with a time of singing, led by a band at the front. I stood when it was time to stand, sang along with the band, sat when told to sit, and followed a programmed service that was consistent from week to week. An offering followed the singing time. A message from one of the pastors followed the offering, and then another song closed the service. The staff worked hard to produce an excellent service. The music was professional. The Bible teaching had depth. Attending the service was uplifting. But when the service was over and the leader dismissed us, I wandered back out to the car, said hello to a few friends along the way, drove home, and had little to do with others in the church until the following weekend when I repeated this scenario. Essentially, the rest of the week, I was on my own.

Meanwhile, on Monday through Saturday, I relished my relationship with the Father. I loved the time I spent with him. The intimacy with him filled me to the full. I treasured the time spent on his lap. But Sunday felt like I was going through the motions. It felt like I was attending a well-orchestrated corporate conference. I could come and go, and I might not even speak with anyone. The service was a well-oiled machine, programmed down to the minute, with cues for the media team on lighting and video projection. Yet, I had almost no interaction on a deep level with anyone. None. There simply wasn't time for that kind of connection in the few moments of the service. As a result, no one in the church knew anything about what was going on in my personal life. They would not know if I had any financial needs. They would not know if I had any health concerns. They would not know if my relationships were falling apart.

In my heart, it felt like there had to be something more.

Around this time, I had the privilege of staying with eight friends at a home in San Francisco for a couple of weeks. We began every morning in prayer together. That morning prayer time was like nothing I had ever experienced. Personally, the time I spent with the Father was rich in connection with him. Now, gathering with others who also had a loving, personal relationship with the Father, the time in prayer was astonishing. We would spend an hour to an hour and a half praying together. We didn't pray around the room. We did not expect everyone to contribute. You prayed as you felt led to pray. We spent little time praying for needs. Most of our prayers focused on what the Father was saying to us. While others were praying, we were listening to what the Father was speaking through them. Someone might play a worship song on their phone while the rest of us sat quietly listening. Someone might read a passage from the Bible. The rest of us would listen carefully, leaning in to hear what the Father was saying to the group. On it went. There were long gaps of silence. At first, the quiet space felt awkward, but it soon became my favorite part of the gathering. In those moments of stillness, I settled in on the lap of God, being held by him.

In those two weeks, I experienced more intimacy with the Father and more connection with other followers of Jesus than in two years of attending a traditional church.

I looked at my relationship with the Father. I wondered if there was a way we could gather other like-minded people together that would encourage that kind of personal connection with the Father. Could we together develop deep, personal relationships with one another and with the Father? Was there a way we could encourage one another on this journey of relationship with the Father, a way to meet one another's needs, to pour our lives into one another for mutual benefit?

I looked into the Bible to see what I could find. It seemed when followers of Jesus met together, there was an understanding of needing one another. There was an understanding that different abilities were given to other people so that when they were living in unity together, the entirety made up a complete body. There was an expectation that each person had something to contribute. The Father, speaking through the Holy Spirit, could speak through every member of the group. They needed one another.

The Gathering

I returned home and began showing others the prayer gathering model we used in San Francisco. I opened up my home for anyone who wanted to attend. After just one gathering, most folks came back because they experienced the Father's presence and love in prayer. The groups grew. Some became stand-alone house churches. Some folks met for prayer during the week while continuing to attend traditional churches on Sunday. Each found deeper intimacy with others and with the Father.

The Father never intended us to live alone. The Father created us to dwell with him, but also with others. He wanted us to follow Jesus with other followers of him. He intended to adopt us into a family, his family, the family of the Father God.

Essentially, a prayer gathering is a family reunion of adopted kids spending time together with their Father. We share stories of how the Father helped us through the week. We share moments of truth he has taught us along the way. We are encouraged to trust the Father more when we hear how he met a need for someone else. And when we stray, we admit it, sometimes reluctantly, confessing our faults one to another, finding solidarity with others who also know the sting. We find healing for emotional and physical needs. We pray together, listening for the Father to speak to us. We pray for one another. If someone in the family has a need, we do all we can to meet it. We sit and talk and laugh, balancing a paper plate of food on our laps. And when finally it is time to leave, it is with a longing for the moment when we will gather again.

And yes, just like any other family, none of our gatherings is perfect. We gather together with all our faults and failings, not as cleaned up, photoshopped, social-media-ready pictures. We are all in different places on our journey to the lap of God. But we are moving forward together. And that makes all the difference.

Suddenly we find we are not alone after all. Throughout the week, we experience the love of the Father individually, meeting with him, sitting on his lap, each one of us believing we are his favorite. Then, when we gather together, we marvel at who he is, his love, his kindness toward all of us. Us. Living, growing, failing, healing.

Together. Sitting on the lap of God.

For more information on the Prayer Gathering model, see the appendix.

*Father of the fatherless...
is God in his holy habitation.*

—*David*
King of ancient Israel

Chapter 20

Sitting on the Lap of God

As I loaded my car with fishing gear and tackle, the sky was just beginning to cast off its blanket of darkness, slowly dissolving into a salmon pink. I drove to the beach before the sun had risen. There were only two other cars in the parking lot when I arrived at the Gulf of Mexico shore. Gradually, the sun crested the tops of the trees flanking the road behind me and warmed my back as I faced the sea. I took a sip of hot coffee from my thermos. A dolphin surfaced in the gulf before me, rays of light sparkling off the smooth gray sides. It had been too long since I spent some time at the beach. It felt like I was visiting an old friend.

As I stood there with the warm saltwater licking my toes, I was struck by how whole I felt. I've been aware of this feeling for some time. A sense of rest has settled into my life. No seeking significance. No journey into the darkest corners of the internet searching for an image to fill the void. No façade to maintain. Just rest.

I thought about how much my life has changed over the twenty years I've lived near this place. The old Tim seems so distant and yet so near. I am humbled when I consider the wandering nature of my journey to this moment. I still have regrets. Yet I feel so much gratitude for the patience and kindness of the Father God and how he has carried me to this moment on the sand.

Once I understood the Father God never intended my dad to fill the Father-shaped hole in my life, I let go of any expectations that he could. The release freed both of us. Fully satisfied in my relationship with the Father God, I now love my dad with the overflow of the love I experience sitting on the lap of God. Just as the Father loves me with all my faults and failings, so too I can love my dad with his faults and failings. Grace upon grace.

I can't imagine how I could be more content than I am at this moment. An awareness of this state has filtered into my mind several times throughout the week. I am resting, perhaps for the first time in my life. There is no striving after wind.

I'm not aware of any unhealthy relationships. I have no interest in pursuing someone to fill an emptiness in my life. I am content. Full. Blessed.

I cannot remember the last time I looked at any porn. Occasionally, like any other man, thoughts enter my mind. I shut them down when I realize I am heading down a path that is deadly to me. There is no yearning to see what I am missing online. There is no sense of curiosity. Instead, I feel a sense of sadness for those who are involved in that industry. If only they could find what I have found. Would they still participate? And I wonder if they know they are loved by their Father.

I could not buy happiness. I now understand it was impossible to buy my way to peace and fulfillment. A beautiful house did not fill the void. Living on a sailboat, following my dreams, did not make a difference in how I felt. Chasing adventures, even a stint in Antarctica, would not fulfill me. Success in the music business or a career in ministry now feels shallow compared with the true love of the Father. Shiny objects can never compete with true love.

I am profoundly happy, filled with joy. I see myself with the Father, his hands lifting me, tossing me upwards, as a laugh spills from my heart. He laughs with me, also filled with joy at the moment. His eyes dance as he looks at me, smile lines creasing his face. "I love you," he says between laughs. "I love you too," I reply, giggling, tiny hands reaching towards his face. I dwell with him, and he with me. I found my happiness in the happiness of the Father, and that has made all the difference.

In this time and place, I am content. I long for nothing. And it makes me smile. I would not trade this moment for anything this world has to offer. I have all I want. I have the Father's love. And it has filled me to the full.

I find wherever I happen to be, I can settle in on the lap of God. This secret treasure is not dependent upon any other relationship. It is not reliant on living in a particular place, experiencing adventures, or anything I could buy with a credit card. Regularly, I settle in for long conversations with the Father. Sometimes I sit there, enjoying his embrace, and no words are spoken. Often words are unnecessary. Always I long to be near him, to dwell with him, aching for home.

It has changed everything. Wounds long revisited, now healed. Façades carefully manicured, now disassembled. Peace. Rest. Wholeness. Complete in knowing I am a child of the Father, sitting on the lap of God.

My life feels like the air after a summer thunderstorm. It is clean, cool, new, refreshed. There is a scent to the air from the ozone released by the lightning. It is still, yet fully alive, exhilarating. In the fullness of the Father's love, I care little what others think of me. I care little what I think of myself. I lose myself in his embrace. It is all that matters to me, his affection, his love, his thoughts of me.

Transformation

I have few words to explain how the transformation in my life occurred. I want to say the Father changed my life through his love, and that is likely true. I have no set of steps to describe the process, the yielding, the surrendering to his embrace, the letting go of personal effort. Instead, it is a singular thing, this sitting on the lap of God, this string of moments of silence in his presence. I repeat the moment over and over, day upon day, month upon month, year upon year. As I do, I long for the moment when I will be face to face with my Father. Someday soon, perhaps.

Again, I turn to the Bible, curious to learn the basic steps for transformation. Surely within its pages, there is a step-by-step guide. Yet, I find no one who transformed themselves. None. Instead, I see many whom the Father transformed. Real, radical transformations couched in the context of complete surrender. The giving up of striving after rest.

For most of my life, I assumed I was unable to change. I unconsciously believed I had an inoperable birth defect. I was born with dysfunctional DNA, and there was nothing I could do about it. I could not imagine transformation, so I settled for discipline to try to manage the situation the best I could. I attempted to discipline myself to minimize the symptoms of my humanity. I gritted my teeth and tried to resist temptation. When I failed, I sought forgiveness from God and vowed to be a better man. I did everything a good Christian is supposed to do, limping along, dragging one foot behind me, striving to live a better life, understanding my limitations.

I held closely to the lie that said I could not change. I could not fathom a life free from shame and guilt. It was all something to be managed. But to be utterly transformed? That was not on my radar.

It is the great lie: we cannot change. Our enemy whispers it over and over, failure after failure. We speak it to ourselves when our attempts at transformation fail yet again. It is just the way it is. Get used to it. Learn to manage it. Our enemy circles about, tracing his finger down the side of our downcast faces, reassuring us, reminding us of our failed attempts, easing our pain with a comforting lie. "That is just the way it is. You're doing the best you can."

Enough.

In every great lie, there is a measure of truth. Our enemy tells us we cannot change. The truth is, we cannot change ourselves. But, my friend, we all can change. There is nothing in our lives the Father cannot transform. Nothing is beyond his touch. Nothing.

Remember, the Bible says, "And such were some of you. But you were washed, you were sanctified, you were justified in the name of the Lord Jesus Christ and by the Spirit of our God." We discovered this earlier when we found our identity in the Father as his sons and daughters. So, yes, we are born with all manner of issues. But all can be transformed in the name of Jesus by the Spirit of the Father in our lives.

The humbling point is to realize the Father transforms me without my participation in the process. The Father did not need me to do anything but to dwell with him. It was in the dwelling, the sitting still with him, that I experienced the transformation I longed for. I spent so much futile effort trying to alter the symptoms; then, in a moment, he transformed the entirety of my life by renovating my soul with his love and kindness.

This transformation is what I want for all of us. I ache witnessing others still limping along, not understanding the love of the Father for them. I shake my head when I see others consumed with the things of this world while the Father extends an invitation to them. He reaches out with both arms, hands wide open, longing to lift us onto his lap. "Come to me," he says, "all you who labor and are heavy laden, and I will give you rest." Rest. Pure, simple rest. All our striving ended, our efforts settled.

It was in the moments sitting on the lap of God that I discovered the Father I always longed for. He was there all along.

The Invitation

Throughout these pages, I've shared my story of growing intimacy with the Father. But the story is unfinished. I continue to write it each time I surrender to his outstretched arms, beckoning me, drawing me onto his lap. Each moment a fresh start, failures left behind, longing looks to the horizon, expecting the sun to rise at any moment and the day to begin anew.

I am remiss to end these pages without a personal invitation for you to join me upon the Father's lap. Nothing would make the Father happier than for you to join me on this grand adventure. He longs for you to dwell with him, to sit with him, sharing intimate conversations. He created you to know him deeply. You are unique, even among the human race, and he knows you better than you know yourself. He knows the beautiful parts – the parts we carefully curate for the world to see – and he knows the places we hide from others. He knows them all.

With one hand, he motions for us to come. As we draw near in curiosity, he leans down and extends the gift of forgiveness to us, the treasure paid for by his Son, Jesus. All our faults and failures paid in full. Every horrid deed accounted for. With wondering eyes, we accept this precious gift. We marvel at its beauty, clinging to it in wonder, holding it close to our hearts with tiny hands. Then our eyes are drawn to the Father's face.

He looks at us and smiles, arms outstretched, reaching, longing, drawing us onto his lap. "Come," he says with a reassuring nod, "I want to spend some time with you."

But he does not force himself upon us. He will not strong-arm us to sit upon his lap. He doesn't demand our attention. Instead, he leaves the choice to us. He stretches out his hand in an invitation to us. He beckons us to come. We choose to accept his love and forgiveness, or we decide to figure out this life apart from his presence and care. It is always our choice.

My friend, will you accept his invitation today? Will you finally let go and surrender completely and entirely to him? Now is the perfect moment to begin. Today is your day! Yield to him. Lay down your burdens at his feet. End the striving once and for all. Find healing long hoped for. Find wholeness. Find peace.

Begin with a conversation with him, acknowledging your faults, failures, regrets. Thank him for the extravagant gift of his Son, paying the penalty for you. Hear the Father say, "You are forgiven," as he smiles at you. Feel the rush of his love, washing you clean, his gentle hands caressing your skin, removing the impurities that stain your life. Marvel as he sweeps you onto his lap, his arms engulfing you, drawing you close to his chest. His love overwhelming. His embrace comforting. His presence secure.

You breathe deeply, like a newborn's first gasp. The air is fresh and clean. Your new life begins.

This is your moment. This is your time.

Discover the Father you've always longed for, sitting on the lap of God.

Acknowledgments

I thank my family for giving me the grace to share my story. This book is my recollection of events and experiences spanning over fifty years that have framed my life and relationship with the Father God. I have done my best to make it a truthful story. Others may look at the same circumstances and have a different recollection. I give grace to those who may see it differently, and I hope I will receive grace from them as well.

I have the privilege of sharing my thoughts thanks to the generosity of many individuals. Joe and Janet Canalichio and Eldon and Lynn Fields assisted in setting up my office for long writing sessions. Wally Metts, Jr., my college English Composition teacher, had the audacity to make me believe I could write. Jennifer Huber, my editor and friend, added clarity to my words with her skill. Carl DuBois edited the material for grammar. Neal and Dee Brown and Teresa Jimenez added additional insights. Jim Gallery proofread the final copy. Rob, Brenda, Tammy, Jennifer, Don, Rhonda, Jacqueline, and David (my prayer gathering family) supported me with prayer and words of encouragement throughout the writing process.

Appendix
How to Host a Gathering

For the most up to date information, please visit timothymark.com.

Host a Gathering Instead of Having a Service

I encourage you to host a gathering of the body instead of having a service. Let me explain. A gathering is different from a service.

We usually think of church as a service instead of a gathering of followers of Jesus. In a service model, we tend to have a set order of events from beginning to end. Usually, we have a time of worship, then a time of announcements and an offering, then a message. The service usually lasts about an hour.

When we have a gathering of our house church on Sundays, we meet together for three to four hours. How can we possibly meet for that long? Because we have a gathering, not a service. Our model is more like a family reunion than a service. Think of it this way. If I have a gathering of close friends in my home, it would seem weird if we all left after only an hour. It would also seem odd if one of us dominated the conversation, and the rest of us just sat there and listened for forty-five minutes. It is the same with our gathering. When we meet together, we are simply a group of close friends who are trying to follow Jesus gathered together. The conversation flows naturally. We learn from one another and pray for one another. We find out what God is doing in each other's lives throughout the week. We meet each other's needs. When we do this, our gathering naturally lasts around four hours.

Since we have a gathering and not a service, it is okay if kids are coming in and out, sitting on laps, or playing in another room. Encourage participation at the earliest age possible.

Have a gathering, not a service. When you gather, begin by caring for one another.

Care for One Another

Take some time to find out how everyone is doing. How has the Father been at work throughout the week? What is the Father teaching you? How do you see the Father at work around you? Learn from one another and encourage one another. During this season, find out if anyone in the group has a financial need. Encourage everyone to meet one another's needs. Pool resources together. What's mine is yours.

Pray Using the Prayer Gathering Model

Have an extended time of prayer together. This is vital. This time of prayer is the one non-negotiable we have each week. We use the prayer gathering model. The focus of the prayer time is to listen to the Father speaking to the group. This is how it works.

1. Assign someone to start the prayer time and someone to close. The one who closes the prayer time should be comfortable with long gaps of silence. A word of caution here is not to close your prayer time down too quickly. Remember to wait on the Father to speak.

2. Do not expect everyone to pray. Likewise, do not pray around the room. Allow each person to pray as he or she feels led to pray.

3. Expect long gaps of silence. Become comfortable in the silence. Remember, you are listening to the Father as he speaks. When he speaks, then you respond. In the silence, listen to him talking to you in your thoughts, then answer in prayer.

4. Respond as others pray. As you are listening to someone pray, something may deeply connect with you. Respond to the Father with your prayer on that topic. Often, the Holy Spirit will develop a theme as the prayer time continues.

5. If a passage from the Bible comes to mind, read it to the group. You may think, "This passage doesn't have anything to do with what is going on in my life." Read it anyway! The Holy Spirit may be trying to speak through you to another member of the group.

6. If a worship chorus comes to mind, play it to the group on your cell phone. Often, worshiping to these songs is as powerful as a corporate worship experience.

7. Sometimes while we are praying, the Holy Spirit may speak to someone with a thought that may be for someone else in the group. This word can be shared either as the prayer time is

progressing or after you have closed in prayer. Never say, "I have a word from the Lord...." Rather, say, "I feel God may be saying this is for you." We always want to speak with humility and godliness. If your group prefers to do this at the end, then after closing in prayer, ask if anyone feels God was saying something to them that might be for someone else in the group.

8. The prayer time ends when the person assigned to close in prayer believes the Father has finished speaking. When I am assigned to close, I just ask the Father, "Are we done?" If he says, "Yes," then I end our time with a closing prayer. If he says, "No," then I wait. Often, God is just getting started, and we shut this time down too soon. Sensitivity to the Spirit is essential. One time I thought a guy closed too soon. It felt like we were just getting started. But I was wrong. I watched the Holy Spirit guide the conversation that followed. The Spirit was still moving. God wanted to minister to a need in the body. It was powerful! So just follow the Holy Spirit.

I encourage you to read these guidelines to the group at the beginning of the prayer gathering, so everyone understands how the prayer time progresses.

And finally,

Share a Meal

We usually have a meal together. There is something about food with friends that binds us together. We keep it simple. The host provides a protein, and the rest of us bring a side dish. No one should feel pressured to make something from scratch. It does not need to be complicated. Hot dogs and chips work!

This model is how God has led us when we gather as a body. This is only a model. There are many ways you can gather. A traditional church may utilize this model in their small group ministry during the week and then gather the individual groups together on Sunday to celebrate what God is doing. The point is to find a way that each member of the family is valued and expected to contribute. We need each other!

Notes

Epigraph: "Is there something at the end of..." q on cbc, "William Shatner opens up about turning 90, loneliness, and what keeps him going." YouTube video, 23:02, April 6, 2021. https://youtu.be/3imVbP_stB4.

Epigraph: "If it's success, you can never..." Marco Sander, "Celebrities on Being Rich But Not Happy (Part 3)." YouTube video, 4:23, August 28, 2020. https://youtu.be/OmWrqelCAJA.

Chapter One

Pg. 5: "The Bible says that God actually walked with Adam and Eve in the cool of the evening." See Genesis 3:8.

Epigraph: "A lot of people say that there's..." Yan Kees, "Alice Cooper on His Christian Faith - (channel: theology Jeremy)." YouTube video, 10:30, May 18, 2021. https://youtu.be/wDWhxeg2F0M.

Chapter Two

Pg. 13: "The Bible says that at the end of all things, God will create a new heaven and a new earth, and the Father God will dwell with us." See Revelation 21:1-3.

Epigraph: "I struggled a long time with..." Goodbye Reality, "Celebrities Talking About Depression, YouTube video, 6:33, May 8, 20212. https://youtu.be/brIJ5OgRI4w.

Chapter Three

Epigraph: "I wish I had had a father who..." The Telegraph, "Barack Obama: 'I wish I'd had a father who was around'," YouTube video, 2:05, February 16, 2013. https://youtu.be/tRQ2yLAGN-4.

Epigraph: "But the gateway to life is very narrow and the road is difficult, and only a few ever find it." Matthew 7:14, NLT.

Chapter Four

Pg. 28: "In my Father's house are many mansions: if it were not so, I would have told you. I go to prepare a place for you. And if I go and prepare a place for you, I will come again, and receive you unto myself; that where I am, there ye may be also." John 14:2-3, KJV.

Pg. 29: "The Bible says we are 'conformed to the image of his Son.'" See Romans 8:29, ESV.

Pg. 31: "Remember, the Bible says the Father would walk with Adam and Eve in the cool of the evening." See Genesis 3:8.

Notes

Epigraph: "There was a sense of still yearning…" Baron, Zach, and Photography by Ryan McGinley. "The Redemption of Justin Bieber." GQ, 13 Apr. 2021, https://www.gq.com/story/justin-bieber-cover-profile-may-2021.

Chapter Five

Pg. 40: "Eight uses in 582,100 words in the English translation." See Kari Lisa Johnson, 'How Many Words Are in the Bible?', https://thewordcounter.com, May 9, 2020, https://thewordcounter.com/blog-how-many-words-are-in-the-bible.

Pg. 43: "My God, my God, why have you forsaken me?" Matthew 27:46, ESV.

Epigraph: "Truly I tell you, anyone who will not receive the kingdom of God like a little child will never enter it." Luke 18:17, NIV.

Chapter Six

Pg. 48: "And they were bringing children to him that he might touch them, and the disciples rebuked them. But when Jesus saw it, he was indignant and said to them, 'Let the children come to me; do not hinder them, for to such belongs the kingdom of God. Truly, I say to you, whoever does not receive the kingdom of God like a child shall not enter it.' And he took them in his arms and blessed them, laying his hands on them." Mark 10:13-16, ESV.

Pg. 52: "The gate is wide and the way is easy that leads to destruction, and those who enter by it are many. For the gate is narrow and the way is hard that leads to life, and those who find it are few." Matthew 7:13-14, ESV.

Epigraph: "Everyone who drinks of this water will be thirsty again, but whoever drinks of the water that I will give him will never be thirsty again." John 4:13-14, ESV.

Chapter Seven

Pg. 65: "And when you pray, do not heap up empty phrases as the Gentiles do, for they think that they will be heard for their many words. Do not be like them, for your Father knows what you need before you ask him." Matthew 6:7-8, ESV.

Pg. 66: "When Jesus teaches us how to pray, he addresses God as 'our Father,' reminding us that we are speaking as children to our Father." See Matthew 6:9.

Epigraph: "The image of the father is..." Bite-sized Philosophy, "Jordan Peterson - Growing Up in a Fatherless Home." YouTube video, 5:08, June 7, 2017. https://youtu.be/zndPSkuyBBk.

Chapter Eight

Pg. 72: "According to Blackaby, the primary ways God speaks to us is 'by the Holy Spirit through the Bible, prayer, circumstances, and the church to reveal himself, his purposes, and his ways.'" Henry Blackaby, Richard Blackaby, and Claude King, *Experiencing God* (Nashville, TN: LifeWay Press, 1990).

Pg. 74: "Do not be afraid to go down to Egypt, for I will make you into a great nation there. I will go down to Egypt with you, and I will surely bring you back again." Genesis 46:3, NIV.

Notes

Epigraph: "I have called you by name, you are mine." Isaiah 43:1, ESV.

Chapter Nine

Pg. 80: "The Bible calls this 'whitewashed tombs, which outwardly appear beautiful, but...'" See Matthew 23:27.

Pg. 81: The story of the temptation of Jesus. See Matthew 4:1-11, Luke 4:1-13.

Pg. 84: "You are my beloved Son, with you I am well pleased." Mark 1:11, ESV.

Pg. 85: "One day I was reading in the Bible what the apostle Paul wrote to the believers in Corinth." See 1 Corinthians 6:9-11.

Epigraph: "We want people to love us..." Rich Roll, "How to Build Awesome Habits: James Clear | Rich Roll Podcast," https://youtu.be/s9uDVVWN_ZE.

Chapter Ten

Epigraph: "We are told that if we're..." Marco Sander, "Celebrities on Being Rich But Not Happy + Giving Advice." YouTube video, 2:09:25, October 28, 2018. https://youtu.be/6Fvmq638E3Y.

Chapter Eleven

Pg. 101: "Jesus even spoke of this in a story he told." See Luke 15:11-32.

Pg. 102: "Father, I have sinned against heaven and before you. I am no longer worthy to be called your son. Treat me as one of your hired servants." Luke 15:18-19, ESV.

Pg. 105: "Stumble." Words and music by Timothy Mark. Copyright 2004 by Global Outreach Music/BMI. All rights reserved.

Epigraph: "Be still, and know that I am God." Psalm 46:10, ESV.

Chapter Twelve

Pg. 110: "As a result, Americans work more hours per week than people in any other country." Stacy Weckesser, 'Americans are now working more hours than any country in the world', bluewatercredit.com, July 21, 2018, https://bluewatercredit.com/americans-now-working-hours-country-world/

Pg. 113: "My thoughts are not your thoughts, neither are your ways my ways, declares the Lord. For as the heavens are higher than the earth, so are my ways higher than your ways and my thoughts than your thoughts." Isaiah 55:8-9, ESV.

Pg. 116: "You are my dearly loved Son, and you bring me great joy." Mark 1:11, NLT.

Pg. 116: "But even as he spoke, a bright cloud overshadowed them, and a voice from the cloud said, 'This is my dearly loved Son, who brings me great joy. Listen to him.'" Matthew 17:5, NLT.

Pg. 117: Story of the Jewish father and the two sons. See Luke 15:11-32.

Notes

Pg. 119: "Depart from me, I never knew you." see Matthew 7:23.

Epigraph: "No temptation has overtaken you that is not common to man." 1 Corinthians 10:13, ESV.

Chapter Thirteen

Pg. 129: "For we do not have a high priest who is unable to sympathize with our weaknesses, but one who in every respect has been tempted as we are, yet without sin. Let us then with confidence draw near to the throne of grace, that we may receive mercy and find grace to help in time of need." Hebrews 4:15-16, ESV.

Pg. 129: "Therefore, confess your sins to one another and pray for one another, that you may be healed." James 5:16, ESV.

Epigraph: "It's always sold as if..." Tiffany Maxwell, "Celebrities share thoughts on anxiety & depression." YouTube video, 7:34, September 5, 2018. https://youtu.be/YIG5mqXpVl4.

Chapter Fourteen

Pg. 135: "The Lord is at hand; do not be anxious about anything, but in everything by prayer and supplication with thanksgiving let your requests be made known to God. And the peace of God, which surpasses all understanding, will guard your hearts and your minds in Christ Jesus." Philippians 4:5-7, ESV.

Pg. 135: "Strong's Concordance defines the word *lord* this way: he to whom a person or thing belongs, about which he has the power of deciding; master, lord, or the possessor and disposer of a thing." Strong, James. *Strong's Exhaustive Concordance of the Bible* (Nashville, TN; Abingdon Press, 1890).

Epigraph: "Even to this day when I..." Rich Roll, "Change Your Brain: Neuroscientist Dr. Andrew Huberman | Rich Roll Podcast." YouTube video, 2:12:41, July 20, 2020. https://youtu.be/SwQhKFMxmDY.

Chapter Fifteen

Pg. 145: "For the kind of sorrow God wants us to experience leads us away from sin and results in salvation. There's no regret for that kind of sorrow. But worldly sorrow, which lacks repentance, results in spiritual death." 2 Corinthians 7:10, NLT.

Pg. 145: "There is a time to cry and a time to laugh, a time to grieve and a time to dance." Ecclesiastes 3:4, NLT.

Pg. 146: "He leads us beside still water. He restores us." See Psalm 23:2-3.

Pg. 147: "His father, Jesse, blatantly showed favor to David's brothers." See 1 Samuel 16.

Pg. 147: "If this was not enough, his siblings verbally abused David." See 1 Samuel 17:28.

Pg. 147: "They assumed the worst of his intentions when he brought food to them on the battlefield." See 1 Samuel 17:28.

Pg. 147: "As an adult, he had an affair with a married woman." See 2 Samuel 11.

Pg. 147: "Then, as if that was not enough, he had her husband murdered in an attempt to cover up it up. See 2 Samuel 11.

Pg. 147: "The Bible says he was a man after God's own heart." See Acts 13:22.

Pg. 147: "The LORD is close to the brokenhearted; he rescues those whose spirits are crushed." Psalm 34:18, NLT.

Pg. 148: "The sacrifices of God are a broken spirit; a broken and contrite heart, O God, you will not despise." Psalm 51:17, ESV.

Pg. 148: "The Lord is merciful and gracious, slow to anger and abounding in steadfast love. He will not always chide, nor will he keep his anger forever. He does not deal with us according to our sins, nor repay us according to our iniquities. For as high as the heavens are above the earth, so great is his steadfast love toward those who fear him; as far as the east is from the west, so far does he remove our transgressions from us. As a father shows compassion to his children, so the Lord shows compassion to those who fear him. For he knows our frame; he remembers that we are dust." Psalm 103:8-14, ESV.

Epigraph: "From working with all the celebrities…" Marco Sander, "Celebrities on Being Rich But Lonely." YouTube video, 4:50, April 17, 2021. https://youtu.be/1ebEIhS0Zms.

Chapter Sixteen

Pg. 157: "The Bible says we have all received 'grace upon grace.'" See John 1:16.

Pg. 160: "Again, the Bible says the Father God knows how he made us. He remembers that he created us out of the dust of the earth." See Psalm 103:14.

Epigraph: "Often, when we describe loneliness…" Marco Sander, "Celebrities on Being Rich But Lonely." YouTube video, 4:50, April 17, 2021. https://youtu.be/1ebEIhS0Zms.

Chapter Seventeen

Pg. 165: The story of the temptation of Jesus. See Matthew 4:1-11, Mark 1:12-13, and Luke 4:1-13.

Pg. 167: "It is written, 'Man shall not live by bread alone, but by every word that comes from the mouth of God.'" Matthew 4:4, ESV.

Pg. 167: "He humbled you and let you hunger and fed you with manna, which you did not know, nor did your fathers know, that he might make you know that man does not live by bread alone, but man lives by every word that comes from the mouth of the Lord." Deuteronomy 8:3, ESV.

Epigraph: "I was a millionaire, I had…" Marco Sander, "Celebrities on Being Rich But Not Happy + Giving Advice." YouTube video, 4:41, May 21, 2019. https://youtu.be/6Fvmq638E3Y.

Chapter Eighteen

Pg. 172: "The Bible says that after the first temptation, then the devil took Jesus to Jerusalem and set him high on top of the temple." See Matthew 4:5.

Pg. 172: "If you are the Son of God, throw yourself down, for it is written, 'He will command his angels concerning you,' and 'On their hands they will bear you up, lest you strike your foot against a stone.'" Matthew 4:6, ESV.

Pg. 172: "Again it is written, 'You shall not put the Lord your God to the test.'" Matthew 4:7, ESV.

Pg. 173: "You shall not put the Lord your God to the test, as you tested him at Massah." Deuteronomy 6:16, ESV.

Pg. 173: The story of Moses leading the nation of Israel out of Egypt. See Exodus 17:1-7.

Pg. 173: "And he called the name of the place Massah and Meribah, because of the quarreling of the people of Israel, and because they tested the Lord by saying, 'Is the Lord among us or not?'" Exodus 17:1-7, ESV.

Pg. 175: Story of the third temptation of Jesus. See Matthew 4:8-10.

Pg. 175: "The kingdoms of this world and their glory." Matthew 4:8, ESV.

Pg. 177: "The greatest among you shall be your servant." Matthew 23:11, ESV.

Pg. 177: "A dispute also arose among them, as to which of them was to be regarded as the greatest. And he said to them, 'The kings of the Gentiles exercise lordship over them, and those in authority over them are called benefactors. But not so with you. Rather, let the greatest among you become as the youngest, and the leader as one who serves.'" Luke 22:24-26, ESV.

Pg. 178: "Then Jesus said to him, 'Be gone, Satan! You shall worship the Lord your God and him only shall you serve.'" See Matthew 4:10.

Pg. 178: "It is the Lord your God you shall fear. Him you shall serve and by his name you shall swear." Deuteronomy 6:13, ESV.

Pg. 178: "'Far be it from you, Lord! This shall never happen to you.' But he turned and said to Peter, 'Get behind me, Satan! You are a hindrance to me. For you are not setting your mind on the things of God, but on the things of man.'" Matthew 16:22-23, ESV.

Pg. 178: "If anyone would come after me, let him deny himself and take up his cross and follow me. For whoever would save his life will lose it, but whoever loses his life for my sake will find it." Matthew 16:24-25, ESV.

Epigraph: "There are psychological needs that are just as valuable and important as physical needs. We know we have needs for..." Marco Sander, "Celebrities on Being Rich But Lonely." YouTube video, 4:45, April 17, 2021. https://youtu.be/1ebEIhS0Zms.

Chapter Nineteen

Epigraph: "Father of the fatherless...is God in his holy habitation." Psalm 68:5, ESV.

Chapter Twenty

Pg. 195: "And such were some of you. But you were washed, you were sanctified, you were justified in the name of the Lord Jesus Christ and by the Spirit of our God." 1 Corinthians 6:11, ESV.

Pg. 196: "Come to me, all who labor and are heavy laden, and I will give you rest." Matthew 11:28, ESV.

Continue the journey.

Join the community at timothymark.com.

Made in the USA
Coppell, TX
04 February 2025

45407718R00139